HOW IS INSANITY WORKING OUT FOR YOU?

Our Guide to Deliberate Measure

By
GB

Copyright © 2023 GB
All rights reserved
First Edition

PAGE PUBLISHING
Conneaut Lake, PA

First originally published by Page Publishing 2023

ISBN 979-8-89157-211-9 (pbk)
ISBN 979-8-89157-231-7 (digital)

Printed in the United States of America

Imagine if you faced a math problem where the numbers did not represent the factual count and symbols such as subtraction and multiplication no longer subtract or multiply. Consider if the variables are revalued daily so even if you know what the values are today those same variables will have different values tomorrow. Do you think there is any way to solve a problem at that point? Even if you manage to solve that problem one day, the identical operations will not solve the same problem the following day. Bogus values give way to bogus solutions. This is exactly what is happening in our society today. Failure is being praised and even exchanged as counterfeit success – and we're supposed to accept this without question.

Don't worry, it won't be all doom and gloom. Personal growth is hardly worth experiencing without some humor and self-deprecation involved. Luckily for us there is plenty to make fun of these days. For starters, many of the so-called, "experts," no longer have the capacity to give a straight answer to simple questions. Seems like every congressional hearing is filled with these sorts which quickly turn potential problem solving opportunities into a standup comedy routine. Basic questions being answered with several qualifying statements followed by pleading the intellectual 5th instead of just saying a yes or no. Many of the sources we count on for accurate information no longer give a complete report of the truth, history, definitions, or unbiased accounts especially involving politics and science. Citing sources anymore is often overrated and counterproductive because many of the sources we have counted on in the past are no longer trustworthy. This is why I do not have Television that has any channels, remain dubious about anything online, and I rarely ever listen to the radio anymore. Whether any of you agree with me or not is not the point of this book. What I am asking of you is to consider each topic through a different point of view. For the past several decades as a society we have tried the gentle touch approach to dealing with serious problems and it has only made the problems worse and created deep paradoxes to try and overcome that shouldn't have existed in the first place.

Whether you like it or not ignoring reality is not going to be an option for much longer. My goal in writing this book is to make you think. I hope to make all of you uncomfortable. I will make a conscious effort to offend every single one of you at some point with facts, personal experiences, my truths, and humor. You may ask yourself why I would do that and the answer is very simple. People who have a reason to be upset can be far more motivated and productive than those who are drunk on bliss or embrace hopelessness as a lifestyle. Personal growth only occurs with honesty coupled with an accurate self-perception. If we do not recognize reality, we'll never be able to accurately access situations and problems, let alone make measured changes to find meaningful solutions.

The first time I recognized this was as a child hearing supposed adults on CNN blame guns for people getting shot and being murdered. My initial thought was something along the lines of, "isn't it the person who pulls the trigger the one to blame?" Without an operator of that firearm, it is just a piece of metal with no mind or ability to do anything on its own. That was the moment I realized some people revalue reality to fit their point of view rather than accept facts. To hold people accountable for their actions and face consequences is a real solution. Holding an object accountable for a person's choices is a bogus value, and thus provides a bogus solution. How's that worked out for the past 35 years?

A few years later I was sitting in a classroom as a freshman in college pursuing a business degree. The professor posed a scenario to the class where your life mission was to climb every mountain with a summit above 26000 feet. After years of struggle and countless thousands of dollars spent you've finally made it to your last mountain, Everest. You only have one chance to climb this mountain – it's now or never. And after weeks of prep and acclamation you're ready to start the climb and fulfill your life goal. Everything is going great and you've made it to camp 2 on the mountain. You start your next day's journey and on your way to camp 3 you find someone badly injured on the mountain. What do you do? You can stop climbing, help them down the mountain, but never reach your life goal. OR, you can leave them there and climb the mountain. They will die, but you will have reached your life goal. Those are your two choices. No radios, no sherpas, no other people to help – this is YOUR choice. After a few minutes of free discussion, he asked us to raise our hands if the choice was to stop and save him. I was the only one who raised my hand. 19 years old and shocked. An older lady in the class (who was a nurse no less) said that she'd find a, "cubby hole," for him on the mountain and, "let him die with dignity." Words I will never forget. In my mind I figured almost everyone would raise their hand and save him. Nope. After the class I had a lengthy talk with the professor. He said that was very typical for everyone to leave him there and finish the climb. We both agreed that in the moment, a lot of people would save him. That was the light bulb moment I realized if a couple layers are peeled back most people are truly out for themselves.

Since then, I have climbed a few mountains. Above tree line everything is different. It can rain without getting anything wet and then it can pour and soak you to the bone. If you've never climbed a mountain before it needs to be on your bucket list. Make sure you are physically prepared, go with a group, know where you are going, never chase your losses, and have the right gear. Keeping your feet dry is crucial too (learned that lesson the hard way). Is there some risk involved, yes. Did I almost see someone earn a Darwin Award by trying to slide off the side of La Plata a few years ago – yup – he just about did a superman off a thousand foot cliff. Would I save you if I found you injured on the side of the mountain knowing this is my last chance to climb – yes, I would and glad to do it. We are beyond blessed to have access to an amazing world meant to be seen with the naked eye.

A few real things you should know about me…

I have XY chromosomes. There is nothing I can do about it. No matter what I self-identify myself as or even if I mutilated myself to appear differently, the reality is I am male. That is my gender and this is a fact. There is no pronoun, medication, or procedure that can change this fact. To claim anything different is a bold faced lie. To expect anyone else to go along with that lie is to expect them to be an accomplice to a fantasy.

I really enjoy playing golf. There are a lot of lessons you can learn from the game of golf about yourself, others, and how the laws of physics work (most of the time). There have been points in time I was really good. But my peaks were never sustained and never at the very, very top. That is reality. If I self-Identified as someone who earned my pro card or has won a major title not only would that be an outrageous lie but it also diminishes the achievements of someone else who has accomplished those feats. Facts do not care about our feelings or fantasies.

You can't cancel me. I have zero social media. I don't have a, "smart," phone. I have no interest in watching tik tok videos because my time is far too valuable to be wasted in self-induced hypnosis without seeking knowledge and perspective. I don't watch porn for several reasons, but the biggest reasons are I value my mind and sexuality. Even if you have dirt on me, I simply don't care. I'm not the hero in this message.

A few definitions we should get out of the way before going further as it pertains to this guide as I understand and define them… And since we don't want these words to self identify, we'll make sure it's filtered through a diaper rather than a dictionary that includes definitions for Gender Fluidity.

1) Words: Sounds that communicate meaning between beings.
2) Deliberate: Intentionally careful reasoning before reaching a conclusion.
3) Measure: A plan to achieve a purpose.
4) Truth: A belief that is commonly accepted. (But can have interpretations that vary from one person to the next)
5) Fact: Indisputable observations about reality that are NOT up for interpretation.
6) Delusion: A bogus belief about external or internal realities which are held despite incontrovertible evidence (those would be facts) to the contrary.
7) Insanity: Doing the same thing over and over again expecting a different result. (I always add in "without changing any of the variables")
8) Woke: Being aware of issues related to racial & social justice. This is just a fancy way of saying useful idiot.

If any of this already makes you upset or uncomfortable embrace that feeling and recognize this is your mind fighting back against years of programming and brainwashing. The level of anger you are experiencing at this moment is an indicator of just how much brainwashing you've allowed into your life. The most productive frame of mind to be in (my opinion) is slightly uncomfortable.

The back story to this has been in the works for a couple years now. I've had two friends kill themselves. They left families, businesses, and decades of life left to be lived unrealized. Their reasoning for making that choice is complicated, and it was their choice to make. Their solution was to deal with temporary problems using a permanent action devoid of hope. It has been other people's consequences to bare. I reached a point a month ago for a couple reasons where I am done indirectly enabling. I'm done sitting back being a, "good friend," just waiting for next phone call to find out someone hung or shot themselves. I am far from the moral police, but it is time to take a stand. I am inviting the spotlight onto my life and those around me. If that is the cost for saving even one person from making that choice then so be it.

My personal path began 11 years ago sitting on a bed 3 weeks after I got married listening to my now ex-wife tell me through her sobs she did not want me and did not want to be married any longer. But it was before that really, I just did not *want* to know it. She'd lost all respect for me long before this point – it was the moment I agreed to commit, to go all in, no matter how she treated me – for nothing tangible in return or meaningful reciprocation. A hard lesson for me had begun which is once someone losses all respect for another, there is no getting it back. I was so blinded by love that I never stopped to consider the warning signs. She didn't have to sell it too hard though because I wanted it so badly. Another hard lesson I would eventually learn was the person who wants it more and cares deeper often receives the scraps (human nature).

I made all the classic, "nice guy," mistakes… Put her ahead of my own goals and purposes, put time with her over exercise and staying fit, put her career far ahead of my own, didn't check her bad behavior, and let that bad behavior worsen over time without any accountability until it devolved into the Springer show. My mistakes were from a place of good intentions. Good intentions without a backbone are just forms of enabling.

One day will be your last. For myself, I have been on borrowed time since 11-4-2011. A bit after 9pm that night I was driving when a truck driven by what I assume to be a drunk came flying around me directly into oncoming traffic. Without consciously knowing it I turned my vehicle into the ditch at 60 MPH while that truck ended up in my lane just ahead of me as the oncoming Cadillac went by so quickly they never even had time to hit their brakes or move out of their lane. I should have died that night. Don't waste this gift of time. You are the legacy of those who came before you and the origin of those to come. My time is coming either way. I have little expectation of dying an old man. I'll be a target whether I make my stand now or let fear and sloth stop me from making that stand later. The difference for me is (my truth) if I do not make my stand now, I will be enabling the destruction of people (many of which being children) that could have been saved. I will not be an accomplice any longer.

A SPECIAL THANK YOU...

For those teachers and staff at schools who really put in the time and energy for the children in their care I want to thank you. For those of you who reject regressive ideologies and activism in the classroom, thank you. For those of you who teach children functional knowledge and help them prepare for an often unforgiving world, thank you. For those of you willing to sacrifice yourself because you love the children in your care, thank you. I was lucky enough to have several teachers in my life who went that extra mile for me and if you are doing that for your students, I applaud your efforts and sacrifices because I know it is not easy. Even if you don't see it now, your efforts will make a huge impact on their lives one day.

To the Police, Sheriff's offices, Fire departments, and Military – you are what keep this country together. We all owe you a debt of gratitude. Most of you are woefully underpaid and then expected to deal with situations that require self control in moments when a normal human reaction would be anything but that. Thank you for your services and sacrifices.

To those who keep our lights on, dispose of our trash, purify our water, provide our energy sources, keep our roadways & transportation systems running, and feed us – thank you for all that you do. Most of you rarely ever get the appreciation you deserve. Today, know that you are appreciated.

Without these people working out of the spotlight we would not have the luxuries we take for granted and the abundance most of us hardly recognize. Right now, it's 71 degrees in here while outside it is 102, on a leather couch, with a bottle of water next to me, with a reasonable expectation of safety, typing away on a lap top, utilizing the gifts of thought that were enhanced by people who gave a shit about me 30 years ago. Tonight, I am going to get in my SUV and drive to the golf course where I am going to work on my putting and chipping, then hit a couple drivers before coming home. Then I am going to walk 2 miles in the dark and when I get home do 200 reps on my mountain climber. Eat some beef and strawberries, take a shower with the temperature I decide at the time that I would like, and write some more. None of this happens without all of you creating these opportunities for me. I live like a king. I've put in the work to have this life, but none of it happens without you making it available for me. Thank you.

So… grab a seat, crack open a Trans Light, and enjoy!

CHAPTER 1

Delusions

When I hear someone say, "self-identifying," I immediately know they're trying to reconcile problems unsuccessfully. Their solution is to make up an insane identity to validate feelings instead of cope with and accept reality. I understand we all experience life differently. The disconnect starts when people begin trying to distort facts to feel better and then expect other people to go along with their daydream. 35 years ago, most of this would have all been deemed common sense. Now common sense has been replaced with voluntary insanity. To question this mass insanity is to commit new age heresy. Time the world gets some tough love and wakes up.

A few years ago, I took a couple family members to Branson, MO for a much needed vacation. When we got there the town was in semi lockdown because the Black Lives Matter folks were having a standoff against the Rednecks of America contingent. Both sides were armed. Both sides were angry. And to me, it looked like the Celebration of Stupidity Pageant was trying to crown a winner. Neither side smart enough to realize that even if they'd had a valid point their behavior and the way in which they conveyed their message means just as much (and sometimes more) than the message itself. Both sides voluntary slaves to masters who laugh at the very causes these people destroy themselves for.

I wasn't sure what the Rednecks were there for except to drink beer and look stupid. I couldn't really understand their message or identify one for that matter, and I don't think they got the hint that the South lost a while back. Celebrating enslavement of other human beings along with a failed economic structure doesn't make much sense to me. Oh, and for the idiot in the old chevy truck who was getting a BJ while driving like it was the Daytona 500 - a word of advice. If you wreck, odds are she'll bite down, and I doubt you can spare losing what she had between her teeth.

For the BLM people… If you really cared about young black men being killed by the thousands then you'd turn the microscope on the inner-city communities and mostly young black men who commit those crimes. You'd ask why there is motivation for violence and destruction. You'd speak out against the collateral damage caused in those communities by that violence. You'd take a stand against real enslavement by way of government subsidy and an education system meant to teach ideology rather than functional knowledge. There are real problems and issues that you could be fighting against. But it is far easier and far more profitable to play the victim. It's far easier to twist a handful of stories of police action to fit a profitable narrative. The message of hope and accountability is the long path. There is no money in it. It means making real commitments to those who often don't want to listen for less than nothing in return. Many of your descendants lived, suffered, and died through hell on Earth. Don't squander this chance to prove that their sacrifices weren't in vain.

Critical Race Theory (CRT) is an idea older than I am. The Theory goes something along the lines of racism is in all legal and social structures and that race is just a social construct and it's all just not fair. It's a whole bunch of belly aching and excuses rather than accepting responsibility for choices and the consequences that follow if you ask me. On one hand race doesn't exist and on the other they claim that all outcomes are because of racism. When I read about CRT, I can't help but think it's the birthchild of delusional people and perpetual victims. I cannot think of a better way to teach racism and division to children than poisoning them with CRT. The intentional replacement of innocence in a child with victimhood, blame for something they have not done, blatant double standards, anger, and resentment is in my opinion a criminal act. A parent trusts teachers and staff at a school with their child's care and best interests. To help teach them meaningful knowledge such as math, science, languages, art, music, history, and sports. Instead of this useful knowledge some teachers and staff infect children with division, hate, and victimhood. The end result is children not excelling in reading, writing, math, history, and science – but feel as though they are victims or are to blame for something they are innocent of. That is child abuse by the teachers and staff who promote and expose children to CRT. It is an abandonment of their authority and oath to those children, parents, and loved ones of those children. I am hard pressed to believe any parent wants their child to grow up ignorant let alone filled with anger or victimhood. I am equally hard pressed to believe any child wants to grow up unable to read, write, become proficient in math, and have no understanding of history while at the same time be a burden to society and their family.

If you ever hear the term, "Inclusion Standards," this is just another way of saying Affirmative Action. Instead of selecting the best option available to perform the task, Affirmative Action/Inclusion Standards desire the selection to be based on gender, race, sexual orientation, political alliance, etc regardless of merit or proficiency. Sometimes even making it more difficult for the, "less desired," groups to succeed. Nothing more than participation trophies for society so the Enlightened can feel better about themselves no matter the eventual consequences. This is discrimination in its purest form.

About 14 years ago I was playing in a handicapped golf tournament. At the time I was a plus 3, so they put me down as scratch in A flight and for some reason I was paired up against a guy who was carrying a 40 handicap in C flight. Meaning on 14 of the holes I was giving him two strokes and on 4 of the holes he was getting three strokes for all practical purposes. We get to the 13th hole and I stuff a 7 iron. He shanks his tee shot 80 yards short of the green, wedges it on, and two putts for a bogey and he effectively won the hole – that was the moment I told myself I would never play in a handicapped event EVER again. He claimed to have had a career day and posted an 88. I shot a 71. I won by 17 but lost by 23. He was rewarded for not being as good (and lying about his actual abilities) as I was while simultaneously I was penalized for having earned the ability to play at that level. Sound familiar these days?

Often the best teacher in life is failure. Participation trophies/awards rob children of failure and the lessons gained from competition. That self-imposed motivation to be better the next time around after taking a loss always made me better. The mindset of participation awards is just another way of trying to guarantee outcomes instead of earning opportunities. This only assures far more people do not excel at anything and continue to repeat past mistakes rather than learn from them. Give children the opportunity to win and lose because competition raises the bar for everyone. As adults, let success and failure sort out your problems instead of depression or pretending that you are a victim. Success can be the best filter for knowing who your real friends are because often the more success you have the fewer the number of people who really want you to succeed. Speaking of Filter, when you hit that wall in life, try listening to, "Skinny," like I do and stay the course. Fair only means you have the chance to earn an opportunity. Fair has NOTHING to do with outcomes. There are few feelings better than quietly achieving your goals despite the efforts of those who try to defeat you.

A young woman who I cared very much about as a young man told me that the year before we'd met, she'd had a one night stand and got pregnant. They decided to get an abortion. The way she told it and how it obviously crushed her ended the debate for me. That kind of regret no one needs in their life. If that baby had been allowed to live, that child would be 24 years old now. Instead, they are nothing but heart ache and regret for a middle-aged woman.

Over 100 years ago the beginnings of Planned Parenthood originated. It was called the American Birth Control League. Margaret Sanger was the founder and a vocal advocate for Eugenics. For those of you that do not know what Eugenics means, it is a term used to describe racial, "improvement," by strategic sterilization and birth control measures used against certain ethnic groups. Their goal was to create perfect human beings on one hand and eliminate groups and ethnicities considered inferior on the other. Sterilization of women of color was being done in the United States into the 1970's. I first learned of this while in college and spent a lot of time reading up on the subject because the idea struck a chord in me. Back then I was still naïve and to an extent innocent. The joining of evil with racism in action to eliminate entire groups of people was and still is disheartening. The Nazi's used a similar concept before and during World War 2. This idea is the foundation for which Planned Parenthood began. Planned Parenthood makes billions of dollars every year. They perform hundreds of thousands of abortions every year. A great deal of that money is tax payer funded, meaning <u>YOU</u> are paying for the death of millions over your lifetime who have done nothing to warrant being exterminated. As a society we should be better than that.

A couple weeks ago I had a conversation with a woman who is completely against the death penalty but is an avid supporter of abortion. She believes that life should never be taken under any circumstances, but that a baby inside a mother is – and I quote – "A Mass of Cells," and is, "Not Viable." I mentioned that, "Mass of Cells," is actually a human being and that person is, "Not Viable," because actions were taken to kill the child before birth. We weren't talking about the instances of rape or incest. We weren't talking about severe medical conditions. For context, we were talking about abortion as a form of birth control. The next logical step in my mind is to determine where that line in the sand is. To her it is a, "Mass of Cells," until birth. But some people are fine with killing a child during the birthing process. Some people are fine with killing a baby days after birth. It is a slippery slope though because once you go down this path the concept of retroactive abortion can extend far beyond birth. It isn't an execution if it's called an abortion. We should all ask ourselves if that is a reality we want to face one day?

The death penalty debate was interesting too. Debating with others who have very opposing points of view is good medicine when done respectfully. She believed that no one should be killed no matter what they've done. She is a warm, kind, caring person who has a good heart but has accepted layers of programming. I brought up Justin Thurber and Dennis Rader as people whom in my opinion deserve to be executed for their crimes. She adamantly said they should not be killed for their crimes. Yet in the same conversation was very much pro-abortion. Kill the innocent product of consenting partners who conceive a child yet spare the individuals who intentionally committed horrific crimes. Selective misplaced mercy for evil yet simultaneously devoid of empathy for babies. An example of what decades of conditioning can do to rob an otherwise good human being of reason and replace it with a narrative. This is a reminder to self reflect from time to time so your compass stays accurate to your belief systems (whether you agree with me or not) because there are forces within our society that would love nothing more than to exchange your values for their narratives.

Since we are on the topic of, "reproductive rights," it is sexually discriminating to deprive a man from his choice with regard to keeping his child or to abort his child. Since he is equally responsible for the conception of the child, he should have equal say in whether or not the child is allowed to live or if the child should be aborted regardless of the woman's desire, right? After all, the baby is really just a, "Mass of Cells," and has no right to life, liberty, or the pursuit of happiness especially in the United States. Whether or not the mother wants to keep the baby, the man should be able to make the final decision just as women are allowed to make the final decision now regardless of biological fact which is only a woman can be pregnant. Anything less is sexual discrimination. The double standards are real – this is just one example. It turns my stomach. Children are our legacy. History will judge us in large part by how we have treated our children. We have replaced logic with double standards – and the tangible price is a literal mountain of dead babies and a lack of accountability to choices. And we wonder why UFO's watch but rarely land… Then consider if a father were to make that choice and it turns out the child was not his, meaning he just killed another man's baby. Another example of how trying to solve temporary problems with permanent solutions creates even bigger problems. Babies are our future, so please consider them as such.

On the death penalty note, my suggestion is an Altitude Chamber where the condemned is placed inside without supplemental oxygen or a pressure suit and the simulated altitude is adjusted to 55,000 feet above sea level where the atmospheric pressure is about 1.3 PSI. The condemned will be unconscious within a matter of seconds and death will occur within minutes. There is a zero percent chance of survival after 30 minutes at that pressure. Makes it a lot harder for legal defense teams to claim cruel and unusual (speaking of twisting what the Founding Fathers actually meant) because we no longer have to worry about flames shooting out of someone's head or the chance that years after execution there is a slim possibility of cancer. Fun fact - above 63,000 feet in elevation the boiling point is below the normal body temperature of a human being (that's bad by the way). We can all get behind this because we're finally using actual science to solve problems.

Since we've dropped in on the topic of science, I get such a kick out of the electric car fiasco. First off, I think my friend's electric BMW is by far the most bad ass ride I have ever been in. It really surprises me that car is street legal considering we went from a dead stop to 60 in maybe 2 seconds. The way I see it with electric versus gasoline/diesel is it's two different ways of getting energy from the same source – and neither is particularly efficient. Both sides work. Neither side is right long term. The theory behind electric cars is primarily burn coal & natural gas (you know, fossil fuels) somewhere else so the emissions are over there. Then we'll throw in a little nuclear, sprinkle some wind and hydro, and just a dash of solar so we can claim the title of, "environmentally sensitive." If you ask the EIA (Energy Information Administration) how much electricity is wasted from production to the point it arrives to you the answer is about 66% (which is probably optimistic). In other words, 66% of the electricity generated is totally wasted and 34% gets to the consumer. Considering some, "green," ideas actually take more energy to produce than the energy they generate and almost all of it doesn't exist without our subsidy dollars, I'll call this a limp W that in reality still relies on fossil fuel sources.

It's hilarious when people claim to be humanitarians on one hand and on the other have no issues with where a lot of the battery components are sourced and refined because we're all set to pat each other on the back for really caring. When we exhaust the resources or the dictatorships stop selling, I'm sure we can call Duck Dodgers and he'll have as much success finding Cobalt and Lithium as he did finding Illudium Phosdex. Only problem there is he won't be available for another 350ish years. I'm sure the disposal of those batteries isn't on the humanitarian's minds either because just like the power plants burning coal and natural gas, the disposal of the batteries is over there so it's someone else's problem to deal with. Never mind the brake pad dust issue versus exhaust system emissions. Once the electric car is all charged up it is much more efficient than the gasoline or diesel-powered vehicles. Getting more than a third of the energy produced at the power plant to the car is the glaring issue. BUT!!!! I have an earth-shattering solution that doesn't involve an Explosive Space Modulator. Let's open up oil production and domestic refining (I get it – not all oils are the same), make energy less expensive, stop relying so heavily on foreign countries that hate us and could easily hold battery components hostage, and start meaningfully incentivizing the invention of real alternatives that make sense. Electric may seem all warm and fuzzy, but it is NOT a long term solution – it is just a money grab with no better morals than buying oil from Venezuela.

Much like a family with a home that has traditions and defined values, the foundations for a country are secure borders and citizenship. Your home has walls and a front door. Your property has a defined boundary. You don't just let anyone trespass onto your property and you don't let strangers into your home without considerations of safety and an invitation after getting to know them. You've established routines in your home for meals, work, paying bills, entertainment, maintenance, education, healthcare, and relationships. The same is true for a country. A country needs defined and secure borders. A country has citizenship for those who are supposed to live there. What is happening at our Southern Border diminishes the value of your citizenship. It weakens the security of our country because we are allowing strangers into it without considerations of safety and invitation.

If the Regressive party (they're the ones that hijacked the democrat party) were truly concerned about the welfare of women and children they'd be completely against illegal immigration. Their policies enable human trafficking and sexual slavery. Their policies open the flood gates for drugs like Cocaine, Fentanyl, Heroin, and Crystal Meth. How many children and young adults (citizens of this country) have to die before we as a people say enough is enough of this? How many children and women have to be sold into sexual slavery here in this country from impoverished nations before we as a people say enough is enough? Why are the, "conservatives," willing to negotiate any of this? There is nothing to negotiate when it comes to sexual slavery and fentanyl being cut into medications or being sold as a street drug. Open border policies endanger the helpless, floods the country with lethal drugs, and dilutes the value of legitimate citizenship for those who were born here and those who followed proper policies to earn their citizenship. This is nothing more than a slow invasion incentivized for political gain at the expense of the very citizens these politicians swore to defend. Elections have consequences and who we have running the show is intentionally destroying this country. There is no justifiable reason to ever vote for anyone who is behind these policies or willing to allow this to happen. As I said before, ignoring reality is not going to be an option for much longer. That time is coming. A vote for them is a vote for human trafficking and drug overdoses by the hundred thousand. You may not verbally agree with these things, but your actions by way of voting support these atrocities if you continue voting for Regressives.

Want a clearer picture of what this looks like up close? I just spent 6 days in Colorado on vacation. An absolutely beautiful state to spend time in nature. However, two of those days were in Colorado Springs. The second evening I filled up at a Circle K gas station and there was a kid no more than 25 years old leaning up against the building. He literally looked dead. A true genetic freak who could have been anything in life, but instead he won't see 30. 2 blocks down from that there were four addicts sitting in front of a business at 6pm. 2 of them were mid-banding up and shooting while I was 20 feet away from them just waiting for my turn to move. Completely out in the open in full view of the public, less than a quarter mile from the nicest part of town. I see no difference between the kid who looked dead but was still kind of alive and my friends who have killed themselves, just that one way takes a little longer is all. To the kid who was trying to die in front of the gas station, your song will always be, "Cast no Shadow," by Oasis to me. I hope I am wrong. I hope you turn it around and see 30. I hope you get your pride back. Spend one day in Colorado Springs and you'll understand this is not a sustainable problem.

On my way back from Colorado Springs, I got a call from the wife of a friend of mine. Their daughter vanished and they wanted to know how long it's been since I'd seen her. They hadn't seen her in 4 days at that point and I hadn't seen her in nearly 2 weeks. Later that day she showed up at their home. She had ran away and relapsed. She's now in rehab and I can only hope she is getting clean. These problems aren't a million miles away. They're down the block, across the street, and up the stairs from you right now. She is lucky to be alive. Many aren't so lucky. If we do nothing it will only get worse. If our public policies continue to promote this it will only get worse. I do not want to think about what my friend and his family have gone through. The parents of the young man half dead up against the gas station. The woman who used to be beautiful but now looks like a skeleton with a needle in her left arm looking at me but not able to make eye contact. As a nation, we can't afford to let many of our young people fall into this nightmare when much of it is avoidable and some of it is even intentional.

On that note of illegal immigration from earlier, does anyone else find it pathetic when a few buses full of immigrants get sent to a liberal mecca and the Regressives throw a great big fit about it? Guess they don't like people trying to escape tyrannical regimes who've walked 1500 miles to end up in sight of their homes, shops, and restaurants – let alone the handful of criminals and terrorists who disguise themselves as migrants. That must be a problem for Florida, Texas, New Mexico, Arizona, and California to deal with on their own because the Liberals sure don't want to deal with it. No need to see that when teeing off at the local club or when they're about to order a T-bone and wine for fear it could ruin the mood.

Where are the Feminists and why aren't they the one's heading up the fight against illegal immigration? I would have thought that they'd have a serious problem with the trafficking of small children and women into sexual enslavement from impoverished nations. Their loudest talking point should be to close up the border and do everything possible to stop human trafficking. Yet, I have never once heard anything remotely close to that from a feminist.

What the feminists never seem to understand is you can't have trans and feminism co-existing long term. Sooner or later, they'll figure out that a, "trans woman," is a just a dude pretending to be a chick. Eventually they'll notice that a, "trans man," is one of their own defecting to the other side. At some point feminists won't want a 6'4" dude with a fat banana in his bikini and a 5'oclock shadow winning all the races and then watching them undress in their locker room. There will come a time when even the most rabid feminists will want a bathroom of their own. Most of all, once guys with nothing to lose figure out that they can just put on a dress and get the societal benefits of a woman and win all the female competitions the feminists will object. And <u>THAT</u> is the moment we will find out which side is stronger. My gut says trans at this point, but I don't have any evidence to support or contradict that suspicion. Just a hunch is all. Maybe it will boil down to which side can hire more male mercenaries to fight their war for them.

There are many people chronically distracted by television, social media, porn, and tik tok. What fantastic ways to self-sabotage and waste away. And not just wasting time and energy, but making it more difficult to communicate and bond with others in a meaningful way. Many times, I have been to restaurants and seen whole families sitting at a table and every single one glued to their phones rather than having a conversation together. Now days many people have a hard time just having a conversation or holding eye contact because they've consumed so much screen time their brain no longer functions without constant digital dopamine hits. For what it's worth, if that is you, try putting the phone down and engaging in a meaningful conversation with a friend or loved one. If you still have great verbal and social skills, this is a reminder to not let those skills deteriorate. Practice makes permanent.

The most counterproductive way, in my opinion, to live life is always trying to be happy and making everyone else around you happy (Guilty as charged). Happy is just an emotion that can come and go from one minute to the next. The pursuit of the never-ending comfort zone creates complacency, laziness, and a deep fear of losing all these comforts that make people think they are their own God. The psychology behind always trying to be happy and comfortable from what I have seen ends in one of two ways – depression or vanity. There are a few traits both vanity and depression have in common that I've seen. Both are terrified of alienation and rejection. Both avoid taking the long path to success. Both chase and cling to emotions for coping with long term problems even though emotions are fleeting and not stable. Both are lazy and look for others to keep them sustained. Both are self-inflicted gateways to destruction. Remember what Dad said about vanity – it's definitely his favorite sin. If you struggle with any of this as I have throughout my whole life, please consider making measured changes to your life so you can avoid these pitfalls. This can be a starting point for a dark path of depression, poor choices, anxiety, and suicide. Please seek help from someone you trust if you see this pattern in your life because it's a far more difficult fight to do alone.

I mentioned God in the last paragraph, so I figured I would give my 2 cents on this subject. My first experience in church was when I was 7 or 8 years old. At the end of the evening the old lady who was running the children's program told me I was going to hell because earlier she had given all the kids paper and asked them to draw pictures. I made a rather nice picture of a monster based off of the movie Predator and she didn't appreciate it too much. Guess she wasn't much of a sci-fi person. About ten years later a close friend of mine convinced me to start going with them. It was a better experience than the first, but the underlying tone of that church was fear. Everyone there was being manipulated by fear to give more money and pray harder. The combination of people being told they'll go to hell for sin along with a transactional relationship with the church didn't make much sense to me. I couldn't buy into that because even as a teenager I was well aware that forcing people to do something long term never works, especially if it's manipulative and rather one sided. Even if most of the message is solid, the way in which that message is conveyed means as much as the message itself. As I got into my later 20's and then my early 30's I had moments where I really believed. But those moments rarely stuck because I was too weak and there were often too many mixed messages for me to ever hold onto one. Too many people who would say one thing and then do another, myself included. Faith is a hard thing for me when I cannot see it – to just trust without concrete evidence. These days I bounce back and forth. The part that I go back to over and over is the idea of a man being crucified and his response to this is saying, "forgive them Lord for they know not what they do." Gets me every time because I know that would be far from my feelings as they pounded stakes into my arms and then decided whether or not they'd break my legs before hanging me up to suffer for days before dying of shock and suffocation. It's the one message and example that has always been constant to me. It has given me perspective several times in my life. I am not going to tell you that you should believe or not believe – that is your choice entirely and I have less than zero authority on the subject. What I will say is that even if you do not believe at all, there is a lot of value from that statement and mindset considering what he was going through in those moments.

It looks like a cell phone, but there have been times I've thought of it as a digital needle. You can call, text, go online, watch movies, check the weather, navigate, etc. with it. All those functions serve a valuable purpose. Over time though, for those who abuse it, their ability to have real in person communication and interactions diminishes. It infects people with a distorted perception of reality. That phone is your diary and it knows you better than you do. Only now, your secrets are not secrets anymore. Don't misunderstand me, advancements in technology are a wonderful thing when used for good. My issue with it comes when leaps in technology occur without the lessons learned from incremental failures and successes, and then those leaps are used by those who are not forces for good often against the very people whom they've sworn to protect.

One Christmas years ago we were all about to eat when through a blue tooth speaker in the living room several of us started hearing a woman moaning. Luckily my brother had the quick sense to get up and shut that thing off before very many people there knew what was going on. It was a young man in my bathroom watching porn on his phone and somehow it linked up to the speaker in the living room. Six months later I had a real talk with him about it. Pornography can be a terribly destructive addiction. It was a struggle for him as a teenager. For myself I have been lucky – it never really did much for me. But for him the moment he was exposed to it the hooks were in. His parents didn't think about controls to his internet access and quickly his online movement went from sports to adult content at an age where no one has the emotional tools to handle what he was exposed to. Parents – this is a reminder to you to monitor what access your kids have online.

That needle is showing its face within your bodies too. Not just in waistlines and depression. Go back tens of thousands of years ago and no one was near sighted. Within my lifetime over 50% of you will be near sighted. We weren't meant to stare at a screen or pages a foot in front of our faces for hours on end. We were meant to look across mountains, oceans, fields, sunsets, and forests. When I go to the lake half the time I have the whole place practically to myself, yet within an hour's drive there are nearly half a million people. Hundreds of thousands of people self hypnotizing themselves within 60 miles, and all those real experiences waiting but never being realized.

If I was trying to kill someone with food, I would use the well-established and accepted food pyramid as a really good starting point. It's not quite backwards, but it is far closer to the worst case scenario than the best case scenario (my personal opinion). A lot of what the FDA lumps into the largest section as I understand the definition does not qualify as actual food. If bacteria won't eat it, why would you? The majority of Americans are now obese and pitifully weak. I have spent a decent chunk of my life in this category and keeping a healthy weight for me is a choice I have to remain diligent with.

There are a lot of reasons for this. Number 1 on that list (besides the choice for the vast majority to be that way whether they want to admit it or not) is diet. The old sayin' we are what we eat is very true.

"Body Positivity," is the result of, "self identifying," and, "participation trophies," merging – thus creating amphibians that live on land but could survive in the sea. Nothing more than the celebration and acceptance of a slow and painful mass suicide. There is nothing sexy or healthy about being 175 pounds overweight and pre-diabetic, let alone trying to force all that into a pair of leggings. For the first time I now agree with reparations because those leggings didn't deserve to have 3 feet of ass explode through what used to be a waist line. If you fall into this category, all kidding aside, please take a moment and ask yourself what you really want for yourself and your loved ones? Please ask yourself if this is the life you envisioned when you were a child? If it is not – NOW is your chance to do something about it. No matter where your starting point is I ask you to start today, because if you don't odds are your starting point tomorrow will be deeper down that hole. Be an example to be proud of. I pray you never find out what having your feet turn black and then being cut off is like – with only death to look forward to. By that point it really is too late. I have had several clients have their feet removed and it is horrible to see, let alone watch them accept as their new reality. Make the changes now so you never face that existence later. Then a final question to ask yourself… Who cares more about you? The, "plus sized community," that tells you everything is fine and you're doing great because misery loves company? Or me - that wants you to escape this body inclusive nightmare and an early horrific death who is willing to tell you the facts because I don't want you to end up in a wheelchair with tubes hanging out of your ass and two stumps where your feet used to be?

Speaking of reparations, I am completely for it. I think it is a brilliant cash grab and I intend to support it all the way to the bank. Let's round up anyone who has a long dead family member from eons ago who either kidnaped, transported, sold, profited, or enabled slavery in any form and liquidate their total assets and then give that money to those who have descendants that were slaves but had nothing to do with human trafficking or profiting from it in any way. I mean, since we are looking for retroactive justice, I have Irish in my family line and to my knowledge no one in my family bought or sold people. How big of a check do I get? Can I get that on auto deposit? In fact, I nominate myself as the modern Robin Hood – I'll steal from the retroactively guilty and give to the descendants of victims. You trust me, right? Unchecked power and the ability to confiscate property without oversight has never been abused in the history of mankind... Oh wait, you mean if we were to do that almost everyone would be rounded up and very few people would get a check? YUP. Once you open the door to this retroactive justice concept it won't stop with this reparation's nonsense. Do we put sanctions on the Germans now for what happened from 1933 to 1945? Do we start bombing Japan again because of the human experiments and atrocities they performed on civilians and POW's during World War II? Do we go after ourselves (all of us) for living here seeing as we displaced an entire civilization? This is nothing more than an extension of the divide, divide, divide until every group is gone all in the name of being equitable. Don't be fooled by these hypocrites – it is nothing more than a money grab with layers of control.

It's always perplexed me when people decide to live in a home that is below sea level. Then they act surprised when it turns out gravity is real and water is wet. After the obvious risk occurs, they sock it to their insurance for their own stupidity (and then somehow manage to complain about insurance claims). Same can be said when people build a wooden house with asphalt shingles on the side of a mountain where wildfires have scorched everything half a dozen times in the past century. Then a wildfire torches their home and they act shocked that their house made of kindling burnt to the ground. Time to have someone else bail them out for their own poor choices. How about when someone decides to purchase life insurance knowing they intend on committing suicide once the contestability period expires, thus making it someone else's debt to pay for their poor choice. Now this mindset has extended far beyond robbing insurance companies. Voting has become little more than an extension of the welfare system plagued by conflicts of interest and

Moral Hazards. When a group or individual makes reckless or self-ish choices without fear of consequences because they think another group or individual will be there to bail them out when the deal goes bad that's called Moral Hazard – sounds familiar these days doesn't it? Voting should be a privilege for those who pay for this country because by paying for it they become responsible for it. With responsibility comes Authority just as parents pay the bills and have authority over their household, not the children. Only people who net contribute to society should have a say in its direction through voting. Those who net take from society like entitled infants have no reason to vote for anything but increasing their own entitlements because they are not taking any of the risks in the process. Beggers should not be choosers. People trying to take advantage of societal nets should not be rewarded for their poor choices by the resources of others. And, there is one huge difference between the insurance companies bailing out people who live in foolish places or commit suicide on their dime and this delusion that everyone should be able to vote. The difference is, the insurance companies knew the risk going into the deal and still accepted the risk and collected a premium for it. Both sides agreed to the terms even if they were ridiculous. Those who net take from society take no risk on their own, pay no premiums, and are incentivized to vote for their own dependence instead of freedom. Only one side agrees to these terms, yet they are still allowed to act on everyone's behalf.

Since we're on the topic of voting my favorite line for this subject is the saying, "Voter Fraud is just good politics." There is no way to know how many times elections have been flip flopped through voter fraud because the system in place now is so convoluted and corrupt. It is literal comedy to me that IDs are not mandatory across the country, let alone who is allowed to vote. Why not just invite everyone to come vote 20 times – once with their own name and 19 times with names from the local cemetery and homeless shelter? Considering there have been instances where voting districts have reported well over 100% voter turnout, for anyone to say this isn't happening now has bypassed deceit and gone straight to corruption. Shout out to Ohio and Florida – thanks for the laughs!

You mad yet? I'm hoping by now at least 95% of you are offended by something I have written so far. Whether it was satire or literal (or something in between), I hope I reached all of you by this point. Even if you agree with me across the board there is plenty to reflect on. With consideration comes perspective, and I hope these perspectives leave you a bit uncomfortable. If you are mad, who are you really mad at?

When I was 36, I started having lower GI issues. Not severe, but enough to know there was a problem. Pretty quickly I realized it was a combination of stress and diet issues. The stress part was an easy fix — that's called divorce. Diet was difficult though, but over time I have trimmed cheese out of my diet and the better I am about it the less inflammation and GI issues I have. Everyone is different though — I mention this because if there is a problem in your body, don't ignore it. Look at your lifestyle, dietary and exercise choices, recovery & rehab choices, see a trusted doctor or actual expert, and make positive changes in your life to get positive results. And remember, it is much harder to regain than it is to maintain.

The healthiest person I know eats NOTHING but unseasoned cooked beef and raw beef liver. Let me guess, you're going to say, "but John, you aren't a diet expert." My response to that is how has listening to the, "experts," worked out for us as a whole? Another thing is that friend of mine is a doctor… Just saying… And unlike the, "Liver King," who relies on large doses of anabolic steroids to get results, my friend truly lives the lifestyle. He completely reversed several serious health conditions, lost 70 pounds, and has the body fat of a 4 iron. If I had to put money on just one person making it to 110 in good health that I know it'd be him. He has been all in for 6 years now and he looks younger in his early 40's than he did in his mid-30's. I am NOT telling you to jump straight into his level of dedication, nor would I lie to you and say I haven't tried to comically tempt him into all sorts of foods like chips and salsa (which, somehow, he never falls for — the man is a rock). What I am telling you is if you are struggling with your physical health, obesity, or have concerning signs of big health problems please don't wait — get it checked out — make informed changes to your life and honestly look at what you are putting into your body. Do not quit smoking the day you get diagnosed stage 4 lung cancer like my Aunt Terry did. Surround yourself with true experts in fitness and nutrition that don't just walk around regurgitating nonsense about having to eat 3 times a day and it needs to be balanced that way you have the proper amount of insecticides in your body to keep your inflammation levels pegged. None of this – any of this – matters if you do not have your health. Life is too long and too short to be a prisoner inside your own body or be poisoned in the name of public health.

Oh, the days of the Triple Lindy. Where there was an actual chance of a useful education without indoctrination at a price tag of 100k-400k. I sometimes try to imagine what it must be like for young people these days going into college. Facing either alienation or brainwashing for years and years only to come out with massive debt and job prospects that often don't fulfill their dreams or pay nearly enough to live on their own or pay the debt they are now anchored with. Instead of learning economics or engineering skills, they learned how to color their hair and hate men or blame themselves for something they never did. Then the government comes out and says we'll forgive all your student loan debt. Then it's we'll forgive 10k of your debt. It took me 14 years to pay off my student loans. I borrowed the money on a degree I have never really used. It was my debt and I was solely responsible for it. If any of you believe this loan forgiveness concept is, "free," then you need a refund instead of forgiveness because all college did was replace your reasoning with a narrative. WAKE UP!

Anytime you hear someone say, "Inclusive," or it is a part of some acronym, remember that word only applies to those who share the same brain fart. Automatically it will exclude free thinkers no matter your beliefs and political ideas and those who operate in reality. If you seek higher truths based on actual facts the, "Inclusive," crowd will not only exclude you, but they will do everything they can to destroy you. The more push back and irrational response you get from these, "inclusive," people the better (from my experience) because that means you're more than likely a force for good who doesn't just automatically conform. Stay on your purposes in life and enjoy their attempts to silence you. Let your success and ability to help others be your response. They will try to separate large groups into small groups. Then they will try to divide each person off of those smaller groups. This isn't just old school divide and conquer, true isolation is their first main target. If you find yourself facing these issues, reach out to friends and family that have your best interests at heart. Find a group of people who make you better than you were and make it easier to stay on your purposes in life. A great group of friends and peers is far stronger than the summation of their individual strengths.

With isolation comes silence. These, "inclusive," people want you to feel alone. They want you to feel embarrassed for not agreeing with their distortions of reality and lies. They want you to be depressed. They want you to give up. They do not want you to speak up when you see children's clothing that promotes trans sexual agendas. They do not want you to publicly disagree with companies and politicians that promote ideals which are destructive to families and children. They do not want you to object to a trans march where they all chant, "We're coming for your children." Their goal is to keep you silent. What they do NOT want you to know is they are a small minority. What they do not want you to know is their ultimate goals have nothing to do with being inclusive and have nothing to do with your long-term survival. If you feel silenced for your beliefs and values, find someone who is vocal and shares similar opinions. Spend time in that space and share your thoughts with them. Grow your voice and stand up for your beliefs.

Not quite 2 years ago I dated a woman for a short while who has a son that experimented with homosexuality even though he is not gay because of social pressures and expectations at his school. A close friend of mine came to me a couple weeks ago and discussed a situation involving his parents and his children regarding pronoun usage and how that is in part causing a deep rift in his family. Compared to many places in this country the area I live in has good schools where a child can expect to receive a functional education. The teachers I've come to know in the past couple years care deeply about their students. Even here there are serious issues people are dealing with.

Families being torn apart. Self-esteem issues and social pressures that turn into choices which cannot be undone and have potentially permanent consequences for everyone involved. None of this happens in a vacuum.

There are two high schools in my region that have kids who self-identify as cats. I refer back to trying to reconcile problems unsuccessfully. I do not know these young people and I do not know their problems which led them to feel the need to exit the human race. I do not know their teachers and I do not know their parents. I can hardly begin to consider the stresses involved in dealing with that first hand. However, allowing such fantasies as coping mechanisms for real problems is absurd. No professional employer will hire them even in a world with, "inclusion standards," if they require a litter box in the bathroom. These children need leadership and boundaries as opposed to enabling fantasies and pushing those delusions on other children. It is hard enough being a child these days, let alone seeing children with severe problems not be disciplined appropriately or receive the help they desperately need at the expense of all the rest. If you are a child with problems, speak to an adult who has your best interests at heart who cares enough about you to tell you the facts and won't lie to you because it might hurt your feelings. Get involved in activities that promote good physical and mental health. Avoid drugs, alcohol, promiscuous sex, and being around kids who commit crimes or behave irrationally. If you are dealing with abuse, go to a teacher or principal who isn't a brainwashed zombie and talk to them. I get that it is terrifying and you're afraid you'll be ignored or rejected at a time when you're most vulnerable. Only you can take that first step. I hope you do. Get help and don't let yourself be isolated and silent because just like the, "inclusive," crowd, the predator relies on your isolation and silence to get away with their abuse of power and authority. Surround yourself with people who actually care about you - ESPECIALLY - when that means they set rational boundaries and expect effort from you in return. If you ever feel like no one in the world cares about you, know that I care about you. I care enough to tell you the facts because I know what writing this book means in the world we now live in. You are NOT alone.

There are men dressing as women going into classrooms teaching children in some schools about anal sex, oral sex, masturbation, pornography, and S&M fetishes right now. Replacing childhood innocence with adulthood behaviors and sexual subcultures. If you fight back against your child being exposed to this obscene child abuse you will be attacked, cancelled, be called a bigot or homophobe, transphobic, sexists, and callous. Pedophiles posing as cross dressers teaching children their perverse sexualities and grooming victims for their own sexual gratification cannot be tolerated in our schools. I call on all of you to put a stop to this because our children's lives are at stake. Do <u>NOT</u> let these forces of evil poison their minds and risk them becoming victims of sexual abuse in our own schools. Schools are meant to be a safe place of learning, not hunting grounds for monsters. Like Karl Childers said, "kids need to have good thoughts." When I think of these children and young adults, I am reminded of, "Nutshell," by Alice in Chains. Their battle all alone, no one to cry to, no place to call home – abandoned in plain sight while these monsters destroy them.

I mentioned evil, so here is my personal definition of evil. There are just two steps as I see it. Step one is a being who intentionally harms another being. Step two is that being then taking great pleasure in the act of harming. The paragraph above is example A of true evil being allowed to exist in our own society.

On a similar note, hundreds of thousands of children are being smuggled across our border due to policies that incentivize this sort of behavior. We are spending billions of dollars to supposedly stop this, yet it's happening on a massive scale. Even after these children get here thousands are lost. How do you lose thousands of kids? People can lose their keys, misplace their wallet, not be able to find a golf ball in the rough… But 20,000 kids and all the government can say is Oops. It's a money maker for everyone involved EXCEPT the children themselves. For them, the most vulnerable of all, they get to experience human trafficking first hand. Elections have consequences, and this is an example of how the wrong people with the wrong motives making intentionally destructive decisions destroy lives in this country and abroad.

Then there are school unions endorsing an administration that openly enables the human trafficking of children and promotes students being exposed to degenerate behaviors by pedophiles in the very school systems these people swore to protect. Their moral compass points directly to the bank so the checks get cashed while their backs are facing away from the children they willfully abandoned. It is more than just corruption. This is child abuse and sexual misconduct against minors. There is no valid excuse to allow any of this to happen. These policies and choices are destroying lives and creating a generation of confused and broken children who will turn to drugs and alcohol as coping mechanisms, many will become criminals, and some will even become predators themselves. There are no good outcomes from this. Most criminals and drug addicts have a background that includes some form of abuse. We now live in a country where there are policies which promote and enable trauma and abuse. Intentionally inflicted because this is a war against our children meant to divide them from themselves before they ever had a chance. I urge all of you to say NO to these forces.

When I was very small there were neighbors in the unit next to us who lived in a nightmare. The father was abusive. He would beat and even rape members of his own family. The cops would show up and they'd claim everything was fine and then the police would go away, only for the nightmare to resume. I remember being 5 and playing right outside my door when the youngest daughter came up to me and asked if I could put my hand down her pants. She was maybe 13. I was terrified and told her no, then I ran inside. From time to time, I would hear what was happening in that apartment. Thin walls don't exactly stop sounds. I didn't really understand what was happening just a few feet away from me, but it sounded like misery. Later that same daughter ended up pregnant. She told my mom that she wasn't sure who the father was because it could have been her boyfriend, uncle, or father. That was my first experience with any of this behavior and even as a small child I swore to myself I would never accept any of that kind of behavior in or around my life. I have no pity for the perpetrators of crimes against children. In my opinion they have forfeit their membership with humanity.

The Trans debate is just silly to me. Tyler Durden said it best when he said, "sticking feathers up your butt doesn't make you a chicken." When a person becomes an adult in this country and they want to live a certain lifestyle I say go for it so long as you aren't treading on others. Want to pretend to be a woman when you're a man or a man when you're a woman – go for it. A lot of people have died so we can live in a society where we have freedom enough to live the way we want so long as we aren't infringing on someone else in the process without the fear of being thrown off a roof top for it. Just don't complain about the consequences of your choices after the fact and don't try to push your lifestyle and identity on anyone else. I will be the first in line to defend your ability, as an adult, to make that choice whether I personally agree with it or not. Where I draw the line is children. Children do not have the capacity to fully understand these choices or the long-term consequences (that is what being a child is – why they need parents). I go back to solving temporary problems with permanent solutions. Children have to wait to become legal adults before voting, buying alcohol, and purchasing firearms. It takes years of experience and growth to fully comprehend what some choices mean and the consequences that follow. The same principal should apply for hormonal and sex reassignment because with time comes the opportunity to make informed decisions and consider consequences. To the, "trans community," I say stop blaming children for your problems and dragging them down with you.

Before you go saying I am transphobic, you should know that I have a trans of my very own. My Katelyn was born factory male, but wanted to be different. So, I pulled out his regular shaft and exchanged his adapter for one that can be set higher. The shaft is an extra stiff now and I can hit her off the tee or from the deck. That was 5 years ago and we couldn't be happier with the transition. And yes, I really do have a driver I call Katelyn. And yes, she's deadly off the deck. Katie off the deck, but they be Bruce off the tee. We can make jokes all day about this stuff – but the reality is there are young people being fed this poison and then encouraged to take medications and undergo surgical procedures that are completely irreversible contrary to what some, "experts," claim. Temporary problems introduced by sick and immoral people onto children who then are pushed to engage in permanent solutions. That looks like a fantastic formula for teen and young adult suicide to me. If you want your children to commit suicide and you hate them to the point you're encouraging them to be mutilated and chemically altered, shame on you! You have no business being a parent. I have nothing but sympathy for children with parents like that. If you love your children and want them to have a fruitful life, keep them far away from <u>anyone</u> who promotes this nonsense being forced onto kids. This is not the time or the subject matter to have your head in the sand. This kind of nonsense only happens if we as a people allow it to happen.

On the note of trans when it comes to entrepreneurial endeavors (because let's face it, no good lie should ever go to waste financially). I'm a bit stuck on my next venture and I'm hoping all of you can help me determine which direction to go. I recently visited with a friend of mine and while on the course the brainchild for the first Trans-wipe was born. No doubt all of you agree not having a trans wipe on the market is discriminatory. He thinks it should be called the Thipe (They and Wipe combined). That's his instinct and I very much agree it is a great idea and really rolls off the tongue well. I'm more of a Tripe (Trans and Wipe combined) kind of guy, although it could be mistaken for an edible wipe which brings us ever closer to a liability nightmare. Any constructive input would be appreciated.

Here's a random question to ask yourself. Some children are allowed and encouraged to get a sex reassignment surgery in their mid teens. Game over for being able to conceive a child for the rest of their lives. Hello to mental and physical problems for the rest of their lives. But adults in their 20's and 30's who are aware of the consequences are often not allowed to get their tubes tied or a vasectomy? Selective hypocritical oaths on blast. I guess we can only sterilize teenagers because they haven't yet had enough life experience to really understand what they are signing up for.

Remember the Defund people? They're the ones that say funding for police departments is a bad thing and their solution to combat crime is to send unarmed social workers to handle criminal activities. They think redirecting funds away from law enforcement agencies and into community programs (more entitlements) is a better way to combat crime and deter criminals. I doubt there are many social workers who want to try and stop an active shooter with a clip board. Social workers often deal with incredibly hard situations, but to ask them to take on the physical role of a policeman is absurd. I would suspect that even the most avid supporters of Defund would dial 911 the moment they hear someone breaking into their home late at night. Criminals commit crimes because they do not respect the law or other people's property and physical wellbeing. Without law enforcement there would be no consequences for criminal behaviors outside street justice. If you think the police and sheriff's departments are bad and due process is corrupt, imagine what a lawless land would look like for a moment and then ask yourself how long you would last in it? Without law enforcement agencies we'd face eventual anarchy. Thank a policeman or sheriff's officer next time you see one because they are there to help protect all of us and our property.

Speaking of protection, the politicians keep harping about gun control. As though a criminal would think about committing a crime with a firearm and later decide not to because there is a law against it. Only law abiding citizens try to follow the law and consider the consequences before acting. These gun control laws are only meant to stop law abiding citizens from legally owning a firearm. The politicians have armed guards. They insist on being surrounded by people with firearms for their own private security. They do not want you to be armed or have the means of effectively defending yourself. What happens when a group of unarmed people stand up to a group of well-armed people? Typically, nothing good for the unarmed crowd. There is a reason why the founding fathers of this nation thought YOU should have the capacity to defend yourself and your property. It is not just a 2nd amendment issue. This concept is a part of the 3rd & 4th amendments too in my opinion. Amendments 5 through 10 have to do with our legal system and the protection of your rights against the federal government. I highly advise everyone reading those first 10 amendments to our constitution and consider why the founders created them in the first place. They did not envision a lot of the issues we deal with today, but they knew all too well the realities of a government that gains too much power over its citizens.

I remember a picture of an Occupy Wall Street guy taking a dump on the side of a cop car. That's the logic of these people. Rather than put together an educated thought or come up with a constructive alternative that isn't backwards, the best they could do is shit on a car and call it progress. This goes back to the BLM and Defund people too – even if you have a valid point, the way in which you convey that message means as much or more than the message itself. When your defining moment is a CNN reporter claiming it is a peaceful protest while cars and buildings are on fire in the immediate background no one is going to take you seriously who can think rationally. Have there been instances of real police brutality and corruption – yes, it has happened. Have there been instances where Wallstreet and our economic systems have gotten greedy at your expense – absolutely. Is burning down a grocery store going to make any of that better – nope. Is raping women going to sway people's opinion to your cause – nope. Your behavior means every bit as much as the cause itself.

My first job after college was as a loan officer. By 2006 it wasn't a secret that the housing market was in deep trouble behind the scenes. There were times I overheard phone calls where an appraiser was asked to value a property with a specific number before they even appraised it. Big surprise the appraisal would come back as requested. To add to the disaster, lenders were loaning up to 120 LTV (loan to value). Then the application did not take into account the applicants' true debts and expenses, so the debt-to-income ratio was always bogus. That created a scenario of appraisals being much higher than they should have been. Then the lender would loan 120% of an inflated valuation on a home that the applicant could not afford in the first place. Multiply that by millions of homes, throw in a lot of speculation and greed, a dash of head in the sand, and you have the 2008 housing bubble. That bubble had been in the works for years. In the 90's there was a big push to lend in lower income areas that changed the way lending was done and who would qualify for a mortgage. In the early 2000's it was the adjustable rate mortgages that doomed the whole thing. Millions of homes and trillions of dollars later and I don't think we've learned a lot because no one was really held responsible. In fact, the consequences were that a lot of the people who helped create the collapse got paid millions in the aftermath while millions of you scrambled for a place to live and to put food on the table. That is why these bozos never stopped – human nature – if you got away with it once odds are you'll get away with it again. They were rewarded for failure. Sets the stage 15 years later for the next collapse and their hope for a bigger payday afterwards. There's a new bubble now, but unlike 2008 where there was collateral (the houses themselves) the new bubble has none.

The new bubble is money itself. 32 trillion plus in debt. The Government can't even give a straight answer on how many trillion in unfunded future liabilities. Inflation rate in reality of 25% to the average person when they go into the local grocery store - not the 9% the fed was claiming. Hell, the COLA (cost of living adjustment) social security added this past year was 8.9%. They never match inflation. Excess amounts of, "money," eventually creates more problems than it solves. The real kicker is the vast majority of that money is not even real – nothing more than a number on a page or screen. All of it is intentionally being done with the goal of controlling you so long as you have utility to their needs. The day is coming where the dollar will be replaced with a Congressional Express debit card that will be issued to you. You'll get an allowance from the government every month that you have to spend because having extra cannot be allowed. Your card will also be linked to your geographic area so your ability to travel will be limited and must be authorized beforehand. Oh, and that pension you've been building up for the past 25 years – what do you think will pay for all of this? That is low hanging fruit for them, and it is always easier to spend someone else's money than your own. Since another goal of the government is for you to not be able to own anything yourself, having financial independence won't be tolerated. Don't worry though, they've already shorted the dollar by now, developed the conversation to their new point system, and simultaneously set the stage for the dollar to eventually collapse. They get all the value and you are left dependent on them. It is not too late to put the brakes on this if enough people say NO, but the point of no return is coming. Far too many of us are walking around with our head in the clouds. It will be sold to you as something for your own good. They know better for you than you know for yourself bullshit. Just trade some of your freedoms for safety. They already had their test run called COVID so they know the response if people are caught off guard.

It is amazing to me that it took so long for people to realize COVID 19 was not the offspring of a bat humping a pig in a cave somewhere in China. Over three years in and we're just now getting little tid bits of information about the lab in China, the funding for the creation of the virus & where those dollars came from, and who profited from it. 7 million people murdered and hundreds of millions of people directly affected and ZERO people held responsible. 7,000,000+ cannot be said enough times. SEVEN MILLION MURDERS. I have lost several clients. Seems like every few weeks I strike up a conversation where someone has lost a spouse, parent, sibling, or coworker from COVID 19 or the, "vaccine." Consider this – a criminal attacks a cop and the police officer manages to shoot the criminal before the criminal can take the police officers gun and kill them with it. That is used to fuel riots and outcry for months. 1 person who was trying to kill a cop gets shot in self-defense by the police officer and people lose their minds to squeeze the situation into a narrative. 7,000,000+ people die worldwide from intentional actions and… wait for it… Not much of anything. The Joker was right – no one cares if it is all a part of the plan. Unless we want this to happen again, there needs to be profound public consequences for those who paid for and created COVID 19. Human nature – doing nothing enables these people to do it again without fear or consideration, each time taking it another step further.

Then there is the miracle, "vaccine," that somehow was developed from scratch in less than a year. There is a reason why medications and vaccines go through a multi-year process before being administered to the public. Human trials alone typically take 5-7 years because it often takes this long to know what the side effects actually are. We skipped steps that have been developed over many decades, and for good reason, to protect people… to protect people (makes no sense at all unless the point is to NOT protect people) … Without knowing what the long-term side effects are… which means the world is now in the actual human trials and we probably won't know what the real side effects are until 2028 or after. Everyone stuck with the same needle without multiple years' worth of independent controlled studies to find out what the side effects are before releasing it to the world.

A lot of the reason for this was to watch our reaction to it. A human psychology experiment of sorts to determine the group level of rational thought when faced with an emergency or perceived crisis. Those who created this mess are laughing their asses off at us. For many people the long-term survival strategy here was to hoard toilet paper, ramen noodles, bottled water, and of all things maple syrup. Oddly makes a little sense because if all a person eats is ramen and maple syrup they'll need plenty of TP once they manage to pass that brick. Wear a mask that does little to stop anything. Keep your kids home and don't go anywhere. Feel like it's your fault when someone around you gets ill rather than the people who paid for and developed the virus in the first place. Get paid up to 1400 dollars a week to sit at home and watch re-runs of Law and Order or family Feud rather than work in the name of public safety. Trade some of your freedoms for an illusion of incremental safety. Exchange self-respect for a pay check. The end result is less freedom and ultimately less safety as well. We took all that money then complain that things are more expensive now… What did we really expect?

Taxes are your single biggest external barrier to independence and wealth both as an individual or as a business entity. ESG is the tool that will be used against us to make sure we stay in line with the modern ideologies. ESG being the acronym for Environmental, Social, and Corporate Governance. This is more of the same woke insanity only now being focused on how businesses can operate with a focus on energy development and usage. This is the government trying to backdoor the discontinuation of oil and coal at our expense. These efforts to replace oil and coal with, "alternative," or, "renewable," sources of energy has nothing to do with the development of real innovation – quite the opposite – and everything to do with making us completely dependent on them. Crude oil refining produces far more than just gasoline and diesel fuel. It also creates tar, kerosene, propane, jet fuel, butane, asphalt, and even some fertilizers we depend on for the food we eat. Almost all plastics come from natural gas. So here is an idea – embrace oil and coal. Turn the economic engine of this country on and incentivize innovation to set the stage for actual, real, cost-effective sources of energy for the next thousand years. Use this as the bridge for something better for transportation and electricity. We live on a giant ball of iron and nickel spinning around a huge fusion reaction. We have access to gravity, electromagnetic fields, and that's right – "Yeah Bitch, Magnets!" Right now, the government is sabotaging actual invention and discovery for political gain at our expense. This is a call for the government to get out of the way and instead incentivize real development of long-term energy sources that make financial and environmental sense.

Guess it depends on the decade whether it is global warming, the next ice age, or when all else fails we'll call it climate change. When the day comes where the Regressives ban Volcanic eruptions and that giant fusion reaction called the Sun from producing heat I'll start buying into their insanity. Oh, and it might help if they started riding bikes and walking instead of flying on their own personal jets. Way to lead by example. My advice is just embrace reality and stop being massive hypocrites. Why not celebrate being wealthy instead of shitting on the successful while simultaneously having your own private jet and being far wealthier than those you condemn? Kinda like Bill Clinton back in the 90's. If he'd just come out and said, "hell yeah she blew me and I've still got it," he would have never been impeached. Lying is what Tripp'd him up. If you don't believe me, ask Hillary because she doesn't think it was an abuse of power. I'm sure Bill would say Me Too. Meanwhile, a special thank you to all the Regressives for giving me so much material to write about. It really is a shame the comedy factor for your insane hypocrisy comes at such a high price for so many.

How is it all our political options anymore look like clowns? Why can't we find a normal human being with all their flaws but

WITHOUT make up and a suit to vote for? I see a suit and I have no trust. I see foundation that was applied with a spoon on a man or woman anymore and I ask what are they hiding underneath all that crap. Just looking for a little humanity here that I can relate to that isn't compromised by foreign entities. I do not expect perfect – everyone has a past. Is it that hard to find a sane, logical, cool under pressure person that can speak from the heart rather than a monitor? With clown shows come the circus… Been a while since we had a non-clown. Oh, and if they went to Epstein Island they're automatically out, clown or not. I don't care how good or bad the policies are – if they abused little girls, I nominate them for an early exile from the human race.

As I see it, there is now a quadruple standard for the law within our country. For most of us we follow the laws in this country and do not consider ourselves above it. We value our freedoms and property. There are three other measures of the law that I have observed now. Measure 1 is the use of the law by politicians against other politicians for political gain or the avoidance of future competition. Early morning raids on homes, officials being held indefinitely, forced to spend unimaginable sums of money for their defense, and reputations being tarnished long before charge or trial let alone any conviction. Measure 2 is politicians being above the law. Bribing foreign governments to help family members avoid prosecution, laundering money from foreign governments that creates conflicts of interest, and covering up or destroying damning evidence – and no one ever facing consequences. Measure 3 is the use of assassination for those who won't be quiet or pose a threat. This does not always mean literal strangulation like what happened to Jeffrey Epstein. This can be cancel culture or reputation assassination. This can mean the invention of bogus allegations that now have to be defended against. Now people's voices can be replicated, text messages can be fabricated, and evidence can be planted in person or digitally. Being framed for crimes is standard operating procedure in the world of politics. All of which creates an environment where knowing what to believe and what is disinformation becomes nearly impossible. Add in the constant bombardment of new scandals and cover ups to the mix and people never have a chance to consider the evidence. Just one scandal and cover up after another. No time to think for ourselves.

Speaking of scandals, it amazes me people bought into the notion that Jeffrey Epstein killed himself yet the pictures of his neck clearly show he was strangled from behind. He did not hang himself – the ligature marks would look much different if he'd been hung. The world is a better place without him in it, but the world would be a much better place if it knew what he knew (and what got him killed). The world needs to know EVERYBODY that went to Epstein Island and the other properties that he procured for celebrities, royalty, executives, and politicians to engage in sexual activity with minors. Jeffrey Epstein had leverage on all of them. Enough leverage to get him killed for it in the hopes that scared off anyone else with similar knowledge from talking or exposing evidence. These people need to face consequences for their actions. They need to be held responsible as we would be if we'd committed the same crimes against children as they did.

Since we are on the topic of pedophiles and politicians, where do you suppose the 20,000 kids, "lost," at the border went? That is the official number which means in reality the actual number is probably much higher. A few may have ended up in healthy situations and simply slipped through the cracks considering 6+ million people have invaded our country in the past couple years. But the overwhelming majority are either being used as sexual slaves or have already been murdered. How can the appetite for small children as sexual objects be so high? How can 20,000 children just get absorbed into the degenerate underworld of our country as though the Earth opened up and swallowed them? In contrast, many politicians and people with the ability to stop this pretend like everything is okay – straight out of South Park, "Nothing to see here," garbage. I'd wager most of those 20,000 children wouldn't say everything is okay. Many of those children can't say anything at all because they were slaughtered by monsters thanks to an administration that enables traffickers to bring them into our country to sell them into hell. If these politicians cared about sex trafficking and the genocide of immigrants trying to escape one hell hole only to be thrown into another one, they'd put a stop to this. Instead, they go out of their way to encourage this behavior. I do not care what they say, I only care about their actions. Their actions prove they want this to happen.

There is a degenerate underworld in this country that prey upon children and women. Nearly equally as disgusting are the people who help these monsters acquire victims and avoid consequences. I've seen it for myself with a now kindergarten teacher who abused a small child at a daycare several years ago. The manager of the daycare and the organization she works for covered it up. She gloated to me a month ago in a Walmart checkout line that he (the now Kindergarten teacher) is doing great, just got married, and her daughter was the flower girl at his wedding. She was so delighted to tell me about how wonderful his life is. The smile she had on her face was a mixture of joy and contempt all rolled up into one. The kind of smile that will stick with you. The kind of smile that will make you write a book and not give a flying fuck what the consequences are.

There are laws against this behavior. Some get caught - most do not. For the ones that do get caught, their punishments are often weak slaps on the wrist compared to the crimes they commit. In my opinion there should be no forgiveness for child predators and rapists in this life or the next, as well as those who falsely accuse such crimes out of spite or rejection. No God is going to forgive them or their enablers. There is no rehabilitation once they've crossed that line. They've elected to exit the human race at the expense of the innocent and vulnerable. This kind of person needs to be stopped at all costs. It starts with NOT creating more monsters at a young age through abuse and indoctrination at home, daycare, or school. Then match the punishments with the crimes so there is less incentivization through the legal system. Most of these monsters were not born this way – they were created through abuses at home or school, substance issues, and their exposure to pornography. If you don't believe me, watch the last interview Ted Bundy gave prior to his execution. Even through his subtle attempts at manipulation he gave real insights into how monsters are created. There is no way to stop it all, but a lot of this is proactively preventable if we as a nation decide to take a stand.

As a group, we are making it easy for the Regressives. Many of them are students of Conflict Theory – as I understand the theory, it is the idea of different groups & society as a whole competing for limited resources and that humans typically look out for themselves thereby conflict will always be unavoidable between subgroups. They are not wrong. However, the issue comes when they use this nature against those they have responsibility for. When this knowledge of human nature is used to create scenarios that increase the likelihood of conflict and scarcity of resources it becomes self-sustaining. Sounds familiar, doesn't it? Beware of anyone who uses the words, "equitable," or, "redistribution," because all that means is stealing your assets. Beware of the incentives that could draw you to that edge and stay aware of forces that might want to give you that little nudge so gravity can do the rest. Situational awareness along with being skeptical of anything that sounds too good to be true can help you avoid the long tumble.

I see three players in our society. They are the Tic Tac Toe players, the Checker players, and the Chess players. The Tic Tac Toe players are the social justice woke idiots who are loud as a default because their beliefs are logically undefendable. Most are incapable of self reliance and often default to violence until there is push back, then they need stress puppies and safe spaces because their response to resistance is always victimhood and excuses. Luckily, this is a minority of our country at this point. They are used as pawns by the Chess players. They're very useful and completely expendable. The second group are the Checker players. This is the majority of people. This group wants to lead a semi private existence and generally care about the law and want to have a fulfilling life and safe community. This group tries to be self-reliant. However, they also have a tendency to be afraid of rocking the boat. They do not want to risk the life they have even if they know the long-term outcome is terrible for their future if they do nothing. They can be conditioned over time so long as the steps are small and subtle. Up until a couple months ago I was deeply planted in this group. The final group are the Chess players. They are a tiny minority who think strategically and have the influence to play out their plans. They position the Tic Tac Toe players to clash against the Checker players. They fuel the Tic Tac Toe players while simultaneously make policy against the Checker players because in their view they know better for them then they know for themselves. They use strategy, logic, and very long-term planning to achieve their goals of dominance and hoarding. They HATE freedom except for their own. They need most of the Checker players to survive and will keep them around once they establish their dominance because what the Chess player does not want you to know is they are nothing more than parasites – incapable of creating anything on their own or surviving without a host. The Chess players do not agree in any way with the Tic Tac Toe players, but see their value to ensure their own power. Once that power is established the Tic Tac Toe players will be hunted down and wiped out immediately because that threat to their power will not be tolerated. This is not the first time this scenario has existed. The result is always the same if allowed to completion. The question is, now that you know the reality we face, what are you going to do about it?

To the Tic Tac Toe players… How is being short sighted, malleable, and irrational working out for you? Would the eight year old version of yourself be proud of what you have become? How does it feel to be a voluntary pawn for a handful of other people who laugh at you and think your causes (while useful to them) are ridiculous? Finally – who do you suppose cares about you more? The Chess players who think you are profoundly stupid and laugh at you and your causes or me, the fellow that cares enough to tell you that your actions are counterproductive and hopes that you wake up before it is too late?

To the Checker players… I know you. I've been you for my whole life. I've been a generally good person who followed the law of the land. I've never stolen anything from a store. Only had one speeding ticket (guilty). Never gone out of my way to intentionally hurt other people. I have made a point to be trustworthy in the businesses I have pursued and take my responsibilities seriously. How has that worked out for me? How is it working out for you? Afraid to rock the boat because it might jeopardize your 58k a year job? Your 258k a year job? We are the ones who have allowed all of this to happen.

You are scared that if you speak up it could risk your pension and reputation. What you fail to accept is that by doing nothing you're giving the Chess players the chance to steal your pension with your blessing. If you allow the Chess players to steal everything you value what good is a reputation? The Tic Tac Toe players are scared of their own shadows – little more than bullies with blue hair who cannot control their own emotions. The Chess players have no power and control but what we voluntarily give them. Both sides chronically helpless weaklings who rely on your fear and laziness to get what they want at YOUR expense. What do YOU care about? Whatever that is, neither the Tic Tac Toe players or the Chess players want you to have it. They want it for themselves and they are hoping you are too scared to tell them no.

To the Chess players… You are using an old play book with new technology. You think you can control the river with a fork. For as bright as you are you're not smart enough to learn from the countless times Communism has been tried. It never works out the way you want it to and more often than not after you've wiped out the Tic Tac Toe players and squandered the resources (human nature – possessions stolen are never cared for or managed the same as possessions earned) you'll be the next ones on the chopping block. You could have been so much more, but you let greed and arrogance mold you into a parasite who plays one group against another until groups no longer exist and freedom is a rumor of days long past. Your legacy is the worst of all. You do not have the excuse of ignorance or the virtue of hard work. You think this time will be different because you have an ace up your sleeve. You think you can control that ace which will eventually be the 4th player. I have no pity for you because you have abused your authority for personal gain at the expense of everyone else. That ace you are counting on will be your master the very day you play it, mark my words.

Right about now a lot of you are thinking I'm crazy and that can't happen here. Communism would never be allowed here and even if it did sink its teeth in, this time it'd be different because we'd give it a new name that sounds nice like Rainbow Universal or the People's Utopia. Let's think about that – Communism does not want you to own any private property. That'd be the, "redistribute wealth," crowd. Communism does not want you to be able to practice religion and hopes you become good little Atheists because Atheists are much easier to condition to things which are self-destructive. The last thing Communism wants is for you to have a moral compass or be a part of a group that holds you to a higher standard. Communism loves the idea of teaching racism, perverse sexuality, modern feminism, and social justice in our schools and implementing these policies in the work place. Broken people are much easier to control than educated people. Divide and conquer until there is nothing left to divide because groups in the end cannot be allowed. Part of why Communism always fails is once they start down this path it always goes too far. The ruler of nothing has nothing. And speaking of social justice, this is the baby step towards distributive justice which will mutate into economic equality. That might sound all warm and cuddly, but the reality is when someone else starts determining for you what you need that opens the door for questions like, "do you serve a purpose?" and, "are you a net asset or a net liability?" to society. You want to see what a bad day looks like – have someone a thousand miles away determine YOU are a net liability to society. The last word you'd associate with that determination is justice. This would be the, "subsidy & entitlement," crowd who want you to become dependent on them for everything from your health insurance, rent, utilities, fuel, travel, food, education, and income – all baby steps towards this end. Want to know who to blame for this if we allow it to happen – grab a mirror and listen to, "Terrible Lie," by Nine Inch Nails.

Communism hates the notion of you being able to defend yourself because that means you might say no. This would be the, "gun control," crowd who only want themselves and criminals to have the ability to fight back. Themselves because they need to control the masses and for the criminals because the masses need consistent reminders why they should not be allowed and cannot be trusted with their own protection. They are counting on a hand full of real victims they created to pull at your heart and sway your attention so they can quietly pursue their goals without being noticed. Communism hates strong men who can lead through example. Communism hates women who are devoted to family and the welfare of their children. People who have strong family bonds and wonderful children have much more to lose and are much more willing to resist infringements on their freedoms and property than those who do not have a good family life and wonderful children to defend. Of all the emotions Communists want you to experience, Hope is the very last one. Hope gives people motivation to be better, to stay on their purposes in life, overcome obstacles, stay physically fit, the strength to stand up for themselves and the things they value, and the awareness to leave something better for the next generation to build on.

This all boils down to a hand full of people wanting to control all the resources and wealth. Nothing more than jealousy and entertainment at your expense. Communists cannot take rejection, but can deal it out with joy – and they take great pleasure in your self-imposed suffering. Remember, none of this happens unless you volunteer it little by little, one step at a time, one exchange of freedom for safety, one exchange of knowledge for narrative, until there is no freedom left and safety is determined by your utility, and your ability to obtain resources is determined by someone else the same way a parent gives their child an allowance only without an ounce of love or empathy.

This Utopian goal has been tried over and over. It has failed over and over. The perfect society does not exist because it is filled with and created by imperfect beings. Yup, that's us – humans. This is why the next logical step always ends up being the attempt at creating perfect beings. There is no way to have a perfect society without perfect beings. Science fiction, right? With enough money parents can now pick from the genetic buffet what traits their children have. Who says there has to be parents to create a child anymore? And why stop there – because even the perfect being can make independent choices, and we can't have that now can we… Best to implant technology into the perfect being so independent thought can be, "enhanced," so these perfect beings never reject their masters. I could keep going because this rabbit hole is endless. It sounds foreign to us, and it's considered a conspiracy theory because for 99% of us we don't live any way like that and wouldn't impose that on others. Most people would rather live and let live. That luxury is soon coming to an end. Every word I have written is the reality we now face if we do and say nothing to stop it. Remember that line I said at the beginning about facts? Facts do not care about your feelings or your fantasies. The good news is we aren't at the finish line yet and it won't happen unless we as a people allow it to. If you like the ideas I just wrote about and think Communism is a winner, then do nothing and say nothing and your dreams of being cared for until you are no longer an asset to the perfect society will come true. If you dislike the reality I just described and think Communism is a giant turd, then resist against these attacks on your freedoms and speak up. Everything I have written about is linked together, and none of it is an accident. Embrace hope and all it entails, that way you can decide your own future on your own terms without anyone else's permission.

CHAPTER 2

Marriage & Divorce

When I think of modern Marriage, I always imagine getting on an airplane with safety pamphlets from Fight Club. Getting on board with a bunch of other dumb suckers looking forward to Fantasy Land, sitting in my seat, and waiting for the PA announcement. The flight attendants go through their checklists as all the passengers cringe and weep looking through the cartoon illustrations of a midair break up and fire engulfed plane crash. Then the Captain comes on over the PA and says, "hello folks, it's 78 degrees outside and perfect skies. The takeoff will probably go pretty smooth but within seconds we should experience severe wind shear. It'll be a bumpy ride for us pilots because we will also be fighting asymmetric thrust and there is a 2 out of 3 chance that we'll have a catastrophic failure at 35,000 feet where the wings will snap off and the vertical stabilizer will disintegrate. At which point the nose of the aircraft will separate from the fuselage and the plane will completely come apart into thousands of pieces while doing about 500 MPH. For most of you death will be instantaneous, but for a lucky few you'll have a couple minutes to consider how much that sucked before hitting the ground at 135 MPH." Then there will be a long pause so everyone can reflect on their decision to board in the first place. At which point the Captain comes back on the PA and says, "Good news though folks, every plane that has ever taken off has landed and we have a solid 1 in 3 chance of landing at our destination utilizing the landing gear the way it was designed to be deployed. If we do manage to get there and make it to the gate alive, most of you will be disappointed with your destination. For a few of you it'll really work out though and I truly wish you the best!" Two seconds later you hear the co-pilot in the background say, "rotate," and everyone starts looking around wondering how they didn't notice that while they were being informed of their future prospects the pilots went ahead and took off.

I should start by telling you I am zero for everything when it comes to intimate relationships. It is entirely my own doing when it boils down to it. Some of it intentional and some of it unintentional. I have spent a lot of time alone and avoided women all together, and I have spent a lot of time "dating" (if that is what it is called these days). What all that failure has given me is knowledge because there is no better teacher than failure. I'm going to tell you a mix of facts and my truths to help you avoid some of the lessons I have had to learn and the consequences I have faced. I have no illusions that you'll like me after this. But, as I will explain later, liking me really doesn't matter in the dating world anymore. Liking me doesn't change reality. Facts do not care about how we feel.

Speaking to my younger audience, most of you at some point will want to have a family. That is a natural thing and the vast majority are preprogrammed to want this. I can tell you from personal experience that being a father is the best thing I have ever done. No matter what happened in my marriage, it was completely worth it. Everything, even this book, is a part of that journey for me. I want a better tomorrow than yesterday and I will not let fear of retaliation for using my past experiences to reinforce reality for you stop me. I'm taking my own advice and speaking out because if I do nothing there is a higher chance there won't be much left when the next generation has their time. This is your chance to look at the mistakes of others, see the consequences, and take action to avoid making those mistakes for yourself. Without question, whom you decide to marry is the biggest choice you will ever make. A wise choice will be a huge asset to both your lives. A poor choice sets you and everyone in your life up for a long road of consequences that you do not want to face or have imposed on others.

I was a very weak husband. I was not willing to speak up when I was tested or call out poor behavior immediately. I had bought into the fairytale that I was supposed to treat my woman like a queen and I thought in return she'd go out of her way to spoil me with kindness, patience, sexuality, and support. I thought that if I sacrificed enough of myself that I could make her happy. The worse things got the more I tried to be nice. I thought if I was extra nice and self-sacrificed enough then maybe she'd change and start reciprocating. This is NOT a pity party – quite the contrary – I did just about everything wrong in marriage. I did not deserve the respect necessary to earn the sort of treatment I desired. Hell, if I'd really looked in the mirror back then I wouldn't have wanted to sleep with me either. Weak men create cruel women. Cruel women create weak men. It is a cycle to be aware of and hedge against.

My ex-wife was much better to date than be married to overall. Even still, there were a few serious red flags that I ignored. I had a couple AH-HA moments and I made the choice to overlook them. Funny part to this looking back now is we got married after only knowing each other 11 months and engaged by month 5, yet I remember feeling so invested. I only knew the parts of her I wanted to know or the parts I imagined. I was making long term choices based on fantasy and incorrect information. Hind sight is better than 20/20. The first AH-HA was only a couple months into our relationship. I was making lunch for her, her roommate at the time, and myself. I was in the kitchen cooking away and out of nowhere she came storming in and read me the riot act. No idea even now what it was about or why she was so mad at me. Her roommate had the look of total shell shock. Completely left field behavior. Then just a few minutes later everything was back to normal like nothing happened. I never called her out on it or asked what it was about. My gut tells me it was some kind of test. I'll take a fat L on that one. What does my behavior and role in the relationship sound like? That is correct – I was more of a chick than my girlfriend. No woman is going to respect a guy who acts like a girl nearly as much as a guy who acts like a man. Women will respect a total douche bag loser over a feminine guy with great intentions almost every time. Right and wrong don't really apply – this is just what it is. This reality is what has created the, "modern," dating & marriage scene.

There is another thing which is a red flag, but comes across much more subtly than disrespectful behavior. The way a woman plans her wedding will tell you how she intends to treat you in marriage. If it is all about that one day and how she is put on a pedestal you need to run Forrest run. If the focus is more on what other people think than your long term needs you need to pull the eject lever immediately. If the last thing she is concerned about are the vows there is a reason why and you don't want to experience that why years down the road. Keep perspective even when there seems to be things that are selfless and ask yourself what is the actual motivation for these choices. In other words, don't be a sucker.

The other glaring red flag was the day before we got married. We'd gone to Sam's Club together for food and supplies for the rehearsal and ceremony. It was a lot of fun and things were going great. We got all the stuff packed into our two vehicles and we were about the head to the location when she pulled up next to me and made the motion to roll down my window. The next couple minutes were a blur. She unloaded on me. No idea what I'd done or why she was so mad when just a minute before we were both on cloud nine. Not sure if it was a test, hoping I'd grow a pair and put her in her place, or if she was trying to get out of it all together. Nope – I went with nice guy and did not stand up for myself at all. I just sat there and took it. We had a really bad rehearsal and nothing seemed to work, and then the next day everything was great and the wedding went as well as a wedding possibly could.

After several hours it was time to head out and consummate our marriage since we'd managed to hold off on going all the way. We spent a lot of time just trying to get all the pins and bead things out of her hair which was super funny. Finally, it was time and I was pumped. For the first 30 seconds it was going so great, and then she locked up and said it hurt. I immediately stopped and did not understand what all was going on. That was the moment she flipped the switch from 95% of the time being caring and kind to no longer keeping up the act. She gave me a taste of what could have been and that was that. Then I got to know the real person I was married to. The one who'd shown her face to me a few times was now who I had to deal with on a regular basis.

I'd never experienced anxiety or depression until I was married. I think it was my body knowing a lot was wrong even if I was not willing to face it. It was a huge weight that made it hard to breathe at times. It made time move very slowly to my perception but sped up the aging process drastically. I often felt like I was in a fog. From just a month into marriage until the day I exited I was shackled by it. Looking back on those days I know that a great deal of it was my own doing because I chose to stay and I chose to put up with it. Down deep I knew I was not being a man. Down deep I knew I was not fulfilling my life's purposes. I'd made the mistake of marrying a woman who was set against me being a man or having success. I was afraid to stand up for myself and my needs. The true definition of bait n' switch and I just let it happen. Over those years I gave up most of my hobbies for her. Down deep I knew there was no way for me to carry the weight of both of us endlessly. That anxiety was my body telling me to wake up. It was my choice to ignore it.

We had some good times too. We took a lot of trips in the beginning and we never stopped going out together. I think in a lot of ways that's what kept it from imploding year one. Intimacy, which I thought was going to be a slam dunk ended up being a brick. I stopped putting in the time I needed into exercise and the married diet was not nearly as healthy as the bachelor diet. I let myself go. Between getting out of shape, being rejected over and over, and the anxiety it got the point where sometimes I couldn't even get it up when I had the opportunity. Even when things went well and I thought maybe this time I figured out the trick, the next day the goal post would move and I'd be rejected. Years went by like this. Sexuality was used as a weapon against me and I didn't do myself any favors in the process. We put up a good front but it was misery for me.

3 years into the marriage and I thought things were getting better. I'd gotten back into a little better shape and we were getting

along reasonably well-ish. It was at this point we decided to make a baby. I was so happy thinking about being a father and a big piece of me thought here is a great excuse to go from getting laid maybe once a month to twice a day (I know, laugh away). We may have dropped the ball for three years, but that night we got it right. To say I was thrilled was an understatement. But then a day went by, then two, then a week, then two weeks – and that was it – back to once a month at best. A piece of me didn't care though because I knew we had made a baby. I knew it. I knew that night. I have never once been nervous about being a dad and it is the best thing I have ever done.

By far the best times in our marriage was the later stages of her pregnancy through about month 5 after she had the baby. There was a stretch there where we finally had what I would consider a semi healthy marriage. We had a great baby shower. There were a lot of good moments. The delivery went about as well as it could have and she was a champ in that delivery room. Our anesthesia guy brought ice cream sandwiches to us that night and it oddly hit the spot. Those were some great times.

Around 6 months after our child was born my ex had a work opportunity she wanted to pursue and, being the foolish but supportive husband, I agreed to it. That entailed me effectively putting my job on hold right when it was starting to take off and being a stay at home dad while she pursued her career. We got a 2nd place and semi moved to that location where she would work 5 days a week while I took care of the baby. I would make my business calls when the baby napped and I went back to our primary residence twice a month to work over the weekend. For a couple months this kind of worked. I was making good money by this point and she was now making great money. Yet I still can't tell you where it all went.

Then came March of 2017. Fifty three weeks to the day after our child was born she told me her intention to leave me so she could live with her ex-boyfriend. Two days prior to this we'd had another failed encounter and she was furious. She called her ex-boyfriend to chew him out for all the damage he had done and how that damage had affected the marriage. Within 24 hours of her contacting him the script had been flipped from her hating him and what he'd done to she was going to move 1100 miles away to live with him at her first opportunity.

For the next two months she went out of her way to tell me how great things were between her and her now boyfriend and all their plans together. It was very surreal because on one hand she was so excited to leave & be with him and on the other she never shied away from saying he was a terrible person. She took great pleasure in hurting me and I just took it – and not just took it but kept trying to salvage the marriage. I never yelled or got visibly mad. I never told her to Fuck Off and go live with that piece of shit if that's what you really want. I remember on two occasions crying which only made her behavior even worse and far more cruel. At one point her best friend at the time came to visit because she knew some of what was going on. She too had done similar things and did not want what happened to her to happen to us. It helped for a day. By this point we were drifting apart and I was exhausted.

A quick lesson to interject with that sadly applies to many women… you can spend years dedicated to a woman, and she will drop you in a matter of a couple conversations with a, "toxic ex," and not even think twice about it. This is why it is so important to know who you're with prior to any real commitment. If there are any horrible exes in their past you need to recognize there is a very real chance they will always be drawn back to that trauma. Their words may say one thing, but ignore the words and pay attention to the long-term choices. The very person they spend years in therapy for is often the one they'll leave you for if given the chance. This is the guy who can string them along endlessly and they just follow like a stray puppy who hasn't eaten anything in four days. Never in a million years would they ever take that behavior from you. Like I say, for the guy they really want there are no rules. Women often become imprinted by the very worst ex in their past. All the more reason to NEVER rush into a committed relationship. Know what you're signing up for before you sign on the dotted line, and make sure the first signature is on the prenuptial. Accountability and defined consequences have a funny way of sorting out a lot of this BS before it even begins. Back to the story and my upcoming moment of clarity…

My moment of clarity came when I snooped on her phone while she was asleep. I'd never done that before and what I found finally woke me up. Their text exchanges were outrageous. They were making fun of me for trying to salvage the marriage. It was finally clear to me that I was wasting my time. From that moment forward I was done. The next couple weeks was planning how to separate and what to do about our parental responsibilities.

The next time I came back home I went to the bank and split up our savings and when I returned, I gave her half plus one dollar. She wanted a different vehicle for the climate she was going to be moving to so I helped her trade off the SUV we had for her newer car. I was happy to help because we were both on the SUV title. The car was in her name only and I was glad to be done with it, so I thought. Don't worry though – no good deed goes unpunished as you'll later discover.

By this point I'd been in contact with her boyfriend's place of employment for over a month going back and forth with them. In his line of work, breaking up marriages is supposed to be frowned upon. For the first several weeks I was solely focused on just trying to get him to leave her alone so I could try and save it. By the time we'd done the vehicle swap and I'd read through some of their text messages I no longer cared about trying to fix the marriage. Down deep I knew that if she left it'd have been the end of her. No matter how I felt about her, the idea of the mother of my child being dead was unacceptable. I worked my way up the food chain of that organization until I finally reached someone who helped put a stop to it. I don't really think any of them cared about the affair, but I do think a scandal would have cost them a lot of money and that is what finally closed that line of communication. I learned a great deal about their line of work from those exchanges.

When the day came to leave I took our child and headed for home. My ex stayed up there and I went back to the primary residence. I remember even before getting out of the city limits going under an overpass and looking right seeing a giant water tower and in that moment I realized my anxiety and stress was gone. Up until that moment I questioned whether I was making the right choice and whether I'd tried hard enough. That relief proved I made the right call. I have not felt that anxiety or stress since. For the next 7 months I was almost entirely the sole caretaker for our child. I took our child back up every few weeks to see mom and the grandparents. My life during that time was very busy and equally relieving. I was able to finally start being me again.

I filed for Divorce in October of 2017. My ex moved back to town in January of 2018 and resumed being an active parent. We shared custody and to say it was a struggle for that first 6 months is an understatement. Seemed like every other day there would be a request to make a change of time or pick up location. Without question divorce has been wonderful. Custody on the other hand teaches lessons a human being is NOT supposed to learn. For as much of a push over as I was in marriage, I was not when it came to custody. I went out of my way to be fair and still do, but I no longer allowed the same unchecked behavior. It's taken years but we now co-parent pretty well. She rarely tries to test me anymore and the part I find funny is she now treats me better than when we were married even though I give her little empathy or attention. I'm semi cold to her and in return she is far kinder. There are lessons to be learned from this paradox.

I've had two different lawyers in the past 5 plus years. The first one wasn't that motivated to help and I was too broken to do much good anyhow. It ended up being shared custody and in some ways I was lucky to get that seeing as so many guys go through the same or even worse and get next to nothing in parenting time. I kept the house, which might sound nice but I think she liked the idea of me not only having to pay for it but also continue living in it since she was the one who wanted it in the first place. I got stuck with the entire credit card bill. The way it was figured as my attorney at the time explained it, the judge looked at the car my ex-wife had and the credit card we shared and deemed them to be of similar debt values. So, she got the car and I got the credit card she racked up. My ex was very much for this. In retrospect I think it was because she was buying St. Louis Cardinals baseball tickets with that credit card for her boyfriend and his co-worker. The idea of me having to pay for his tickets no doubt was something she rather enjoyed. It took me 18 months to pay off that card.

On the subject of money, an odd thing happened though along the way. All of the sudden it was a one income household. The bills were actually higher than before by a little, plus I was paying a couple hundred bucks an hour for an attorney... And all of the sudden I had money again. I still don't fully understand how that all worked and at this point it doesn't matter. But the lesson is invaluable. Trust your gut and keep an eye on the budget because if things stop making sense there is a reason.

It was during this stage that I was on a walk around town when I happened across a woman who was also on a walk. We started talking and walking together that day. We had plenty to talk about seeing as she was dealing with similar circumstances. We exchanged numbers after a couple hours and went our separate ways. My mind was still struggling and wasn't at all thinking about seeing someone. That night way late I got a multi volume text message from her. The cliff notes version was she wanted to be FWB. I politely said no and thanked her. I just wasn't in that space. I think between my rejection of her request and our shared circumstances that only made her want me more. Over the next couple weeks she adopted the, "if you don't succeed – try, try, try, try, try, try – again model," and eventually I caved. That first time being with her I was scared, paranoid, and unsure of myself at first. No doubt a few people I know will absolutely not approve of what I am saying, but it's the truth... That night changed my life. I got my man card back. Any notions that I was the problem or that there was something wrong with me was completely thrown out the window. It was exactly what we both needed physically and emotionally. We shared real conversations. We shared real passion. There were no pressures from either of us. We had our time together and eventually that time passed. We ended the relationship on a really good, mutually agreed note. Looking back, it is oddly the healthiest relationship I have ever had. To you, thank you.

For the past 4 years since I have dated on and off. Tried different dating sites on and off. I have spent a lot of time single and there have been times I have seen as many as four women simultaneously. Some I have been willing to consider commitment to and some there was no circumstance I would ever commit to. There have been times I have looked at relationships with women as little more than a psychological experiment. I never disillusioned them about it or hid the fact I was seeing multiple women when that was the case. I have been lucky to be in the category where being single is a choice and recognize for most men having even one option is lucky let alone having multiple options and the luxury of at times being able to say no thanks. The lessons I learned and the realities of modern dating I'll be going into later on. I'll leave it here with a final note that it's been everything from fun, eye opening, fascinating, confusing, and disappointing. Like I have said before and I'll say it again, I am not the hero of this story.

Soon after my ex moved back she started seeing a guy. To say it was a struggle for me the idea of him staying overnight with her while our child was there is an understatement. Luckily, she has good taste in men and in a different scenario I could see him and I being friends. The only knock on him I have is when my kid comes home and tells me about how they argue in front of all the children. Not cool, but also not a whole lot I can do about it. So, it is a learning opportunity for me to provide a different household and environment with no drama and no wild emotional swings. There isn't enough money in the world for me to ever want to go back to that existence.

In 2019 my ex and her then new husband wanted to buy a home. I'd tried unsuccessfully for over a year by this point to refinance the house because being self-employed I couldn't qualify (oh the days of 2006). She was having a hard time qualifying too because she was on the note as well. At one point she came over to my house and in the driveway told me I needed to find a cosigner. I looked at her and said, "I already have one – it's you." I don't think she'd realized that. I'd made about 30 straight payments for both of us by this point and no doubt it'd made her credit score golden just like it'd done mine.

Right after that I was served papers by a very nice lady regarding the house. My ex was trying to force the sale of the home long after the divorce so she could get a new house with her new hubby. We went round and round on this. Finally, it was time to go to court. I had proof of perfect payments and we had agreed in the divorce I would keep the house. I was supposed to refinance the home, but was unable to. She was still on the mortgage, but I was confident I would win. Her lawyer contacted me via email the morning of court and said I did not need to show up. That got a good laugh out of me. I thought about the list of people I trusted on planet Earth and neither my ex or her lawyer were on it. So, I called the county court and asked if I needed to be there. The lady who answered probably thought I was stupid for even asking and said yes, I definitely needed to be there. I printed off the email from her lawyer along with all the other documents I had and headed to court a bit early. Court is quite an experience – I highly advise avoiding it. Anyhow, when her lawyer got there the look on her face when she saw me told me all I needed to know. It took about 30 minutes to have my name called and when it was her lawyer made a dash for the bench without even asking. She whispered to the judge for maybe 10 seconds and BAM, case dismissed. Lesson here is NNNNEEEVVVVEEEEERRRRR trust an ex or their lawyer, because they were counting on me being the, "nice guy," and just going along with it. Meanwhile, I get a warrant out for no show to court and they win the case outright. I face going to jail and they sell the house out from under me – thus setting the stage to go after custody immediately after. Oh, and have paper copies of EVERYTHIING!!!!! You cannot have too much documentation.

About a year after this I get a call out of the blue. A friend of mine had just found out his spouse was having an affair and he was furious. I spent the next 45 minutes talking him out of making some poor choices. I told him what happened with my marriage and how it affected me. How I knew exactly what he was feeling. I eventually got him calmed down and convinced him there is no need to grab a shovel to help morons who are already digging their own holes. Then an interesting thing happened. He told me the events and facts I told him about my divorce was about a 180 from what my ex had told everyone else. Not that I was really that surprised. A lot of things started to make sense to me as I thought about that conversation in the following days. How people treated me. How some people even looked at me. It's a bit ironic too considering one of the people who refuses to even make eye contact with me is one of the people who was that close to having a very bad day. I see the affair partner around town sometimes and he is completely oblivious – straight up space cadet. Now days when I see the man who called me he seems genuinely happy and his life is in a great place. He made the right choice. He opted to NOT use permanent solutions to solve temporary problems. He used logic and reason rather than emotions and anger to deal with the situation. He is now receiving the positive consequences of those great choices. I could not be prouder of him.

Then came 2021… A great year and a terrible year all in one. My ex and I were working well together overall. She was living in her new home and was putting roots down. She had decided to move very close to the school our child was scheduled to go to for kindergarten. Super convenient for me too at a little over half a mile from my home. I was finally breathing a sigh of relief and was in a really good place. Until I wasn't…

The divorce decree I signed back in 2018 was the third version. The first two version forbade my parents from being able to see my child at all. No justifiable reason – looking back I think it was an extreme measure to use as a bargaining chip for what they really wanted. There was also a big push for my child to go to school several hours away starting in kindergarten. Now I had to negotiate the custody of my child and at the same time the ability of my parents to be able to see their only grandchild. The first lawyer I had wasn't much help. I eventually agreed to the school 3 hours away so my parents could see their own grandchild.

Then June 2021 rolls around and she tells me they've decided to move after all and they want to exercise the custody agreement we'd set in place even though just weeks before she'd enrolled our child in the local school and now lived within a 6 iron from the grounds. Instead of 3 hours away they wanted to move 45 minutes away. I basically told her to pound sand and that was NOT going to happen. She was welcome to move but our child was going to stay with me. I then received the vilest letter of my life from her officially stating their intent. No doubt a lot of it was coached by her lawyer the way it was worded. I took 24 hours to calm down, then I wrote a response telling her exactly what would happen and then went lawyer shopping. This time around I got the best lawyer a man could hope for. I did not care what it cost and I didn't care I was partially going back on an obscene agreement that she was semi-trying to exercise. I was not about to just let this happen. There was way too much on the line because I knew if she won my kid would get bounced around all over creation and maybe into some lefty school system. That man (my lawyer) went above and beyond for me and my child. A couple words of advice… One, keep records of everything. Two, be proactive and don't wait. Three, listen to everything your lawyer says assuming they're on your side. Four, when it gets to this point do not communicate in any way with your ex outside your lawyer (we'll come back to this one). Five, get rid of any distractions in your life when you're dealing with a mess like this. Keep your life simple and avoid any stresses or pitfalls. And six, do not make any decisions if your emotions are bouncing around. Try to stay calm and remain focused on the hand full of things that actually matter and disregard the BS.

The day of court came and we were ready. My ex was pushing for primary residential custody instead of the shared custody that we had been doing since January 2018. Going to court and watching how each side presents a case for their client is a real learning experience. One of the big lessons I learned from court was first listen to your lawyer and give them as much accurate information as possible prior to ever stepping into court. I had kept detailed records on multiple calendars of everything related to custody exchanges and schedules going back into 2017. I also kept several letters from my ex which later came in quite handy. Another thing that stood out to me was my ex's testimony. She told the truth for the most part and was honest about things that many people would lie about, but then was not honest about a couple things which didn't seem very important in comparison. Lesson there is be honest even if it looks bad because the lies about the relatively inconsequential things brings into doubt the rest of the testimony even if it is the truth. There was one thing the other side could have done but for some reason did not even though they threatened to before the day of court. My ex had kept the text exchanges we'd had for the past several years. There were times I lashed out at her for behavior and choices which could have been presented in court. I was more than happy to defend every word I wrote (my guess is they did not open that can of worms because I was more than eager to speak at length about those messages). The lesson is why put yourself in that scenario when it does not change the outcome? The secondary extension of the lesson here is do NOT text in anger or resentment, whether justified or not, because there may come a point where you have to defend something you wrote from months or even years prior. In other words, if it's important then send it though a lawyer. Otherwise, calm down and send short constructive messages that cannot be framed any other way. Finally, if the judge asks for a couple weeks to weigh the evidence before making a decision keep your life as simple as possible and avoid any sudden changes – basically keep it completely on the straight and narrow. My ex went directly from court that day and closed on her new home 45 minutes away not two hours later even though the judge had not ruled yet either way. It proved she was moving regardless of the ruling. I think that is what tipped the scales my way and a couple weeks later I won primary residential custody.

I was allowed to be flexible with the schedule and give her more time when I saw fit. Over time it has gotten easier and we've gotten better at co-parenting. I give her much credit for not being outwardly mad or resentful for how court went. The distance at times has been an issue, but we've made sure to go the extra mile (literally) so that it can work as smoothly as possible. I make a conscious effort to be generous with the schedule, per my lawyer's advice, and in part because it is also important for our child in the long run. I have to remind myself at times to stay vigilant when there are long stretches of good times because getting complacent and lazy with keeping records is not an option I care to explore. My text exchanges are short and to the point. It's important to stay prepared for the future. I've been to court 3 times in the past 6 years. Odds are I will be in court again if history is any indicator.

I've told you the PG-13 cliff notes version of my marriage, divorce, and courtroom experiences for a reason. It is not to drag my ex through the mud. I made plenty of mistakes and for a very long time and was a weak, soft excuse of a man. For both men and women, I tell you all this as a reminder to NOT rush into marriage. I tell you this to look at dating as purely sunk cost and never over invest your emotions or resources. I tell you this because it is VITAL you test drive before you buy. I tell you this because you need to know the realities of your future spouse's past prior to saying I do. I tell you this because once you sign that paper you're committed. The wedding is just one day. Marriage is supposed to be for the rest of your life. Who you select as your spouse is the biggest intersection of your life. Do NOT ignore red flags. The best case scenario with red flags is they are testing you. Worst case scenario is those red flags are really what that person is. Both scenarios will result in disaster. I was wrong for her and she was wrong for me. If you think it will get better after Marriage, I am here to tell you that is not the case. If you make the mistakes I made you should not expect a result any different than what I experienced.

CHAPTER 3

The New Divide Between Men and Women

The old saying men have been taught how to treat a woman but not what to expect from her, while women are taught what to expect from a man but not how to treat him is truer now than ever before. Human nature assures that power without consequences is almost always abused. Men are being incentivized to become feminine and women are being incentivized to become more masculine. And remember what I wrote earlier – weak men create cruel women and cruel women create weak men. This is at the heart of so many of the problems our society has now with divorce, suicide, the inability to bond, substance abuse, and hopelessness. For many men time is moving too slowly and for many women time is moving too quickly. Modern society has created this paradox which is making life and relationships far more difficult for the average person.

Use this chapter as a checklist for red flags as well as self-assessment. Sometimes the best lessons are learned by knowing what NOT to do as well as what to avoid. Almost all the problems I see and have experienced are voluntary choices others and myself have made. Then we as a group tend to not reflect and learn from our mistakes sufficiently enough to avoid repeating them. It's easier to say it was the other person who was completely in the wrong. We repeat the same patterns of behavior over and over again, this time thinking it'll be a different result, yet we didn't change any of our own variables – just the person in front of us. How's insanity working out as a culture? We know what the consequences are because none of us are re-inventing the wheel and we know how it rolls. This is my attempt to either remind you to stay diligent or wake you up so we as a people stop repeating the same mistakes.

I still believe in the theory of marriage. The problem is trying to filter it through what has happened to our society and accepted values (mine included). It's hard to build a house on a broken foundation. Even more difficult for that house with no foundation to survive the storm. If we want any of this to work, we have to start by building foundations that can support the home and survive the storms.

I think the error most men have made within my lifetime is they (myself very much included in this) have chosen the path of least resistance for problem resolution. Many of us have forgotten how to be a leader. Many of us do not command respect amongst our peers and within our own households. Many of us have let ourselves go physically which in turn creates insecurities and hopelessness. Many men allow obvious lies and delusions to persist without calling them out. It is easier to enable and ignore problems than to take a stand and prohibit irrational behaviors no matter the personal consequences. Many men have allowed fear into their lives. They are not willing to compete because they're afraid to lose even though they are consciously aware not competing guarantees perpetual loss. Some are unable to compete because they have chosen to be physically and mentally diminished from what they should be. Men should not shy away from competition, but instead embrace it. Men should be humble in victory and embrace loss without anger or resentment. If any of this rings a bell in your life, please start taking steps to rectify these shortcomings. One of the beauties of being a man is we can be appreciating assets so long as we continue pursuing our goals and stay focused. We can determine our own value. It is almost never too late to reinvent yourself. The day is coming when the world will need strong men once again to save the day.

Hello ladies… You were probably thinking this was all about bashing women, but it is quite the opposite of that. I am going to list 5 generalized types of men to avoid. All 5 kinds of men are weak even if on the outside they seem strong. All 5 kinds of men I describe do NOT have your best interests ultimately at heart even if some of them aren't intentionally destructive. Like I basically said earlier, good intentions with bad results doesn't really make the outcome any better.

1. The first one is the most obvious but often the hardest to get away from. This is the guy who is so insecure that he resorts to physical, emotional, and sexual abuse. Why he is this way should not concern you. Have **ZERO** pity for him. Get yourself and your family as far away as possible from this kind of person. I know what this kind of person looks like and how they manipulate and create co-dependency traps for you to fall into. Don't believe a word they say. This is the guy many of you can fall for the hardest and will re-invite back into your life years down the road. Find help and get out of these situations because they are relying on your self-imposed fear and isolation. Then reflect on how you'd gotten into that situation and remember that you now have real baggage and real triggers. Question for yourself now is are you going to carry that baggage, or is it going to carry you? Are you going to learn from your mistakes and the consequences you and your loved ones have now faced or will you repeat these same mistakes if given the chance in the future?

2. The second one is the guy who has no ambition or drive to succeed and relies on others for his survival even though he is able bodied. A lot of guys who watch an excessive amount of porn or play video games for hours on end fall into this category. Time wasters who are not focused on accomplishing the things they need to be working on. This is not the kind of man to have in your life when the chips are down and you need him to come through. If he is unwilling to

prepare for and hedge against hard times when things are easy then the hard times will crush him. He may try to be there for you, but odds are he will fail because the only training he put himself through is repeated and intentional failure so there is no reason to expect different results once pressure to perform is added. People generally default to their level of training in all things. If his level of training is laziness and failure you do not want to go along for that ride.

3. The third one is the, "nice guy," who does not stand up for his own needs and/or keeps perspective on what matters within the household. This is the guy who would rather avoid confrontation all together than call out bad behavior or problems and then deal with them constructively. This is the guy who is incapable of leading the household and will not earn the respect necessary to run it long term. He is concerned about how you feel and just wants to make you happy even if that means enabling terrible behavior. This is the easiest guy to cheat on. The poly chicks love these guys. I know this man all too well because that was me. Like I said earlier, good intentions with bad results doesn't make the outcome any better.

4. The fourth one is the complainer who is never happy and always shifts blame and responsibility to others. He is absolutely opposed to accepting consequences and refuses to learn from his errors long term. Typically, this kind of person is a combination of immature and cowardly. These are also the kind that tend to have unhinged jealousy issues and want to control where you go and what you do. This is the kind of guy that can graduate from this to category 1 if things get heated enough. They are solely out for their own good and will not be there for you when the chips are down. A big piece of being a man is accepting responsibility for choices and not shying away from the consequences, good or bad, that come from those responsibilities. Men who throw fits and complain are not men at all. This is the

second most dangerous man on the list because he has no control of his emotions, nor will he stand up for you when the time comes.

5. Finally, number 5, is the man who does not take care of himself physically. For the vast majority of men, the decision to be weak and overweight is a choice. Most men these days can't do a single pull up. Most men have a far larger waistline than chest measurement. Most men do not have any form of self control with their diet and make excuses on exercise. Is that the example you want for your children? Is that what you as a woman want to bounce on at night? Is a man who can barely do 10 pushups the guy you want to defend you if someone is trying to harm you and your family? Is this the man you want to see deteriorate mentally as he gets into his senior years because he didn't care for his body? If he doesn't care enough about himself, why should you really expect him to care about you? That is not the recipe for a leader who will earn and maintain your respect.

To each of these 5 kinds of men, a word of advice.

For the first kind of man, I have no pity for you. You've abused your authority and responsibilities. You've decided to physically harm, sexually abuse, and intentionally damage women emotionally and often their children as well as a means of control and problem resolution to make yourself feel better. 4 years ago, I dated a woman who'd gone through this kind of treatment for 16 years prior to meeting me. She could not handle healthy intimacy or respectful conversations. She wanted to be treated poorly. That was all she knew. Guys like you create baggage that carries women who could be incredible and prevents them from pursuing healthy relationships. Karma will hopefully sort you out.

For the second kind of man, after you read this go to the mirror and just look at yourself for 5 minutes without sound or thought. Then ask yourself are you proud of what you've made yourself into? Do you respect yourself? Do you really have anything to show for your life greater than yourself? Because when you say no, consider that if you are not proud of yourself and you don't have any respect for yourself why would anyone else? Women respond to strong men whom they respect, PERIOD! If this isn't you, find constructive means of earning self-respect. Make yourself into something to be proud of. Find a means of training yourself to be a better version of you. Work on something that is bigger than you are. Even if no one else notices, the next time you look in the mirror you'll know. That confidence and self-respect you've earned is contagious.

For the third man, you are going to face an uphill battle because just like me you were brainwashed into believing in unicorns and rainbows. You're the guy that tries to treat others the way you wish to be treated. In a perfect world that works, and if you manage to meet the right woman who is aligned with that philosophy young enough it can work because she will give you the unconditional support and trust needed to maintain this thought process. Odds are though you won't meet her. Odds are you'll become a doormat because broken women are looking for you. There is nothing wrong with being a pleasant, humble human being. The problem is you are led by your emotions rather than your common sense and you're not strong enough to defend yourself or your responsibilities. You would rather be walked on than hurt someone else's feelings. This is a very feminine mindset and women do not respect it at all. You may have good intentions, but if your results are poor then stop the insanity and start changing some of the variables you have control over. Time to value yourself enough to not allow others to walk on you. Get your priorities in line, get strong, surround yourself with confident men, and call your own shots rather than being someone else's bitch.

The fourth guy is a tough one because this mentality is deeply engrained more often than not from childhood. Complainers and people who avoid consequences for choices at all cost have a hard time facing the reality that they have created their own problems. Until this kind of guy gets a grip long term on his emotions and develops the ability to reflect without blaming others he will be stuck in this rut. Be mindful when you escalate and control your emotions. If this is you, I would advise joining a combat sports club for 3 reasons. First, you'll discover very quickly you are not God. Second, they will drive home the value of discipline because blaming anyone else but yourself for shortcomings will not be tolerated. Third, you'll get into shape if you stick with it long enough.

Finally, the fifth man… This is a majority, sad to say. You may be a couple of the ones listed above plus this. Even if you have it together across the board except for this, sooner or later your physical inabilities and deterioration will catch up to you. Remember what I said about your level of training? If your training level is zero and then you face health issues your lack of discipline and willpower will prevent you from overcoming what could have been avoided in the first place. No one makes it out of life alive, but there is no need to speed up the process and be a burden to yourself and others for years and years. I have two gyms personally, go to another friend's gym weekly, hit the park playground a couple times a week, and have a membership to the local weightroom (that I barely use). You are only as strong as your weakest link. There are a lot of things that we have no control over, but your physical fitness is something the vast majority of us have some level of control over. I have a great friend who has serious lower GI issues, multiple blood clots, just overcame cancer, terrible side effects from medications, and had open heart surgery just a couple years ago and he still lifts every day. He is in his 60's and still pulls 315 off the floor for reps and can still do reps with 225 on the bench weighing 185. He has a plethora of excuses to stop. In 22 years, I have yet to have heard one come out of his mouth. Without lifting and staying physically fit I would have gone to his funeral years ago. He is a man who commands the respect of many without needing to ask for it. What is your excuse?

You thought I was going to list players on here, didn't you? The thing about players is to get played you have to go along with it. If you don't play with the player he can't play you. There are always warning signs with them. You know better instinctively, so don't complain when you play ball with one and he burns you. If you make this choice it is entirely on you. The only knock I have on players is most of them aren't honest about how many women they're seeing or that you're disposable after they get what they want. To the player, just tell them straight. Most women don't care if you are seeing other women so long as they respect you enough, I assure you. In fact, the vast majority of women will want you more if you have other options so be completely upfront about it. And if she is pursuing you knowing you are a player, she doesn't want strings down deep, she just wants to get laid. They want it every bit as much as guys do, they're just pickier about whom they do it with is all. The lie is, odds are, 100 times worse than the thing that you lied about – keep that in mind.

There is a sub set of player to be <u>very</u> careful of… It's a player with a dash of evil. If you're the kind of guy that gets off on the lie, then that is a whole different ball of wax. To you, there is no need for me to grab a shovel to dig your hole – you're doing a great job – and sooner than later odds are you'll be in it. This is the guy who targets wives. The reason being is wives are often far easier to hook up with than single women. Anyone triggered by that? Don't believe me? Your local bar and dating apps are full of wives. Single women have, "standards," whereas many wives are just tired of the same ole' same ole' and when they get the opportunity, they'll go buck wild. Most of them have friends that encourage these behaviors. Most of them will blame alcohol when they get caught. Don't feel bad for these women though – they knew what they were doing. Don't feel bad for the player who knew she was married either – he knew what he was doing too. They both will get caught soon enough and they will both face consequences for their choices in the long run.

There is also a kind of man who is intentionally incapable of commitment under normal circumstances. Most of these men have been made by cruel women. Some of them are just wired that way because ambition overwhelms any desire for romance. The why really doesn't matter anymore. They may become the most attractive man to you in time even if they are not now because they have learned through failure what it takes. They have embraced competition and self-reliance. If you pursue this kind of man recognize that odds are they will not commit to you. That doesn't mean they won't be loving & caring partners so long as you reciprocate equally or greater, but realize it will probably never materialize into a ring and you will have to initiate contact most of the time. So long as you stay level headed and allow them to lead without resistance you'll probably be able to maintain some level of relationship. If you test them or lose it emotionally, odds are your relationship with them will be over. You'll be hurt and he won't care. Consider yourself informed if you make that choice. I know this man because this is where I have existed for some time now.

Ladies, another thing to watch for is whom your man spends his time with. Just like you, whom a man surrounds himself with is whom he will tend to become a composite of. Success breeds success just as lazy breeds lazy. Also, how his peer group treats their significant others plays a huge part in how he will treat you. If his peer group, in general, is supportive of their wives and girlfriends' odds are he will be supportive of you. If they are not, then you should keep that in mind before getting too involved.

Guys, whom your wife or girlfriend spends her time with will often tell you who she is. My ex's best friend when we met ended up cheating on her husband at the time. If your girl is close friends with party girls, bar hopers, OF models, or cheaters the odds of her being any different are slim. Oh, and if she says she's doing a, "girl's weekend," and then is distant during her trip but then when she gets back all of the sudden she's love bombing you for no particular reason… Guess what… That isn't because she missed you. That's just a spontaneous moment of regret for what went down during her trip. Trust your gut and your taste buds.

Here is some reality for you. People cheat. Women cheat more than men. Why? Because it is far easier for her to cheat than it is for him. Most women have no clue how much game a man has to have to see and maintain a relationship with two women, let alone three or four. Absolutely no clue. That is because for them having 2 or 4 or 10 guys in their roster is average now. When I meet a woman, I automatically assume she is seeing 5 guys at that moment. She may only be banging one or two of them, but I do not remember the last time I actually met a truly single woman. It probably exists, but like the Tasmanian Tiger, it may have gone extinct a few decades ago. Most men have zero options. Even if they want to cheat, they simply have no access. If a woman wants to cheat, she can go to the local bar or get on tinder and within two hours she is in business. Very, very, VERY few men have these abilities. The best looking most successful man cannot compete with a totally average looking woman when it comes to who can get laid easier. Doesn't make it any better, but these are facts. Best advice I have is try to be honest and let the chips fall where they may. If you are in a monogamous relationship and want to cheat, just break up with them first. Simple. Problem solved. Drama free-ish. Stop wasting the other person's time and emotions.

Let me guess – I'm a misogynist, sexist pig, and the final boss of the patriarchy, etc. OR, should we just act better? Is presenting facts sexist now? Most everything I am writing I have learned from experiences with women, so if you want to get mad look squarely in the mirror and say, "how dare you teach him to see reality for what it is." Speaking of, thank you for showing me the nature of women and in that my own nature. Knowledge gives all of us the ability to avoid dangers and seek better options.

Facts for us to all agree to… Men are success objects and women are sex objects. No – then why do we insult men by calling them losers & bums and we insult women by calling them sluts and hoes? Because our instincts know these facts even if we as a society frown upon reality. Women start losing value in their 30's right at the same age when men start to become valuable. No? Then why do women get so mad when they are replaced by a younger, sexier woman? Because they know down deep, they don't have as much value to give and on top of that they know they expect more in return. Women are often judged by their pasts while men are often judged by their potential future. In part why in my 40's I can attract way more women, put in way less effort (often no effort), and get far better results than when I was in my 20's? I looked way better at 22 than 42. I intentionally present the world a parody display because it goes against the grain, and even still I have options. I've been laughing my ass off about it for years now.

So, what changed? I think it is a combination of several things. First, in general, monogamy is mostly dead. No, don't believe me? Think we don't need a chocolate covered miracle pill in the dating and marriage scene? Then go ahead and hop on your spouses' phone, email, credit card statements, and social media without them having a clue. Then hire a PI to follow them for a month. A few of you will find nothing suspicious. The majority of you will find behaviors, inappropriate relationships, and people in their lives you are not comfortable with. Human nature is being enhanced with social media and dating apps… Access has changed the game. Second, unbalanced competition has created a giant void. I have news for you – the vast majority of single women (and a lot of married women too) are sleeping with a small percentage of the men. Why? Because only a hand full of men fit the ladies' checklists and have the attitude and fitness to back it up. Most men now are too feminine and weak to make a woman wet. Men are trying to become soft passive chicks and it's not working. Third, most women are now giving less and expecting more for it. Their expectations and self perceived values are way out of whack while their behavior is far worse. This is why a lot of men are just stepping away and saying they're done with the BS. They're tired of a shitty deal where they have to give the max to receive a minimum, only to get dumped years down the line and be stuck with the bill. Or, they just look at most women as recreational use only. The answers are simple – don't lie, be a man, and give a quality deal that represents reality. If all else fails, say Humperdinck and move on.

On a note of effort, in the past year I have experimented with different levels of effort to verify that my assumptions were facts. I was not disappointed. Last year I went out of my way to NOT pursue anyone seriously, would take hours to respond most of the time, and gave little in terms of effort. In return I was pursued constantly, and often by multiple women even though I made it clear I was not going to commit in any way and often said no to advances and offers. For the past several months I have made a point to take a few minutes each day and text bomb someone who has in the past been interested in me. I know, you'd say that's not cool – but it was never going to work anyhow. And the responses have been either nothing at all or very short and often hours of waiting before hearing anything. Same women – very different results and actions. GUYS! Stop over pursuing women. They absolutely do not respond to it.

Now days I am so bold that for the past two years I will ask a woman practically out of the gate if she has ever been in a threesome and how many men she has slept with in one day – point blank. Do you think any of them get mad? 20 years ago, it would have ended every date instantly. These days they are so desensitized that now they ALL think it is hilarious and they ALL tell on themselves. They have all (except for 2) told me they've been in threesomes and the lowest number I have been told was 2 guys in one day. The highest was 8 dudes, although one lady (who was pulling down 300k a year at the time) told me that in high school she had serviced most of a football team at a party. We'll call that an outlier beyond the 4th standard deviation (I hope). If I didn't have the personality and the balls to straight ask most of them would say, "never and 1." That is reality. A few would tell the truth no matter what, but most will lie through their teeth unless they feel safe enough and are having enough fun to divulge such information. NONE of them are sweet angels. Her career, religious background, income, education, fitness level, personality, looks, claimed values – none of it matters as far as I can tell anymore. I assure you that the vast majority have done things you cannot comprehend and under no circumstances is she going to tell **YOU** about it, especially if she sold herself to you in the beginning as semi-innocent and un-pummeled. A solid half have either been swingers at some point or been involved in sex parties. One told me about having been a prostitute in the past. Several have told me how they've scheduled guys back, to back, to back while laughing their asses off about it. Another told me about a group of women who rent out banquet rooms at hotels and organize cum shot parties where they all cheer each other on while getting facials from strangers under the disguise of girl's night out or girl's weekend get aways. That is what empowered looks like now. Suppose the husbands and boyfriends would be cool with that empowerment being sprayed all over their girl's faces?

A short message to those who organize said cum shot parties… Asking a mostly lesbian if she'd like to spend a hundred dollars so she can go blow some random dude and have him blast her face with a load of empowerment while all of you cheer it on isn't the greatest game plan. Just sayin'. Then again, without your stupidity I wouldn't have had hours of laughter at your expense. When you get caught by your husband or boyfriend the only person you have to blame is in the mirror. I can just see the double standards now… your dad is disappointed in your behavior and that is acceptable, but when your boyfriend or husband leaves you for doing things with a rando that you won't do with him he is toxic and part of the patriarchy. So funny! This whole empowerment through self degradation thing is moral cancer to our society.

Want to really get an eye-opening experience. Start a group chat with a couple women you are seeing. That's a lot of fun til it's not. I thought I knew what women think about and how they operate. NOPE. Let you guess which two these were, and for perspective these two had a better moral compass than most I've met and still their inner thoughts blew my mind. That was a window into the souls of women I will **NEVER** forget and men are not supposed to see under any circumstances. Truly a backstage pass. If they respect you enough, they have absolutely no rules. It was doomed to fail from the start – I knew that and so did they – human nature. They both knew about each other prior and had no problem with it. But once they met it was just a matter of time because jealousy is something even respect cannot overcome. Add in mixed signals. twisting timelines, and at different points each of us considering real relationships and it's nothing more than a time bomb. Being bi-sexual and bipolar at the same time is really an interesting combination to have in two women. Jealousy brings out the worst in people, and alcohol doesn't help. They knew going in it was an experiment with an expiration date. Easily the greatest learning experiences of my dating life and I learned where the line in the sand needs to be for me on that one (semi-retirement). Changed my life… To both of you, even though you might not accept this – thank you. Proof that you can't seriously pursue multiple people if you intend at some point being committed to one.

This brings me to another topic which is open marriages and swinging. I knew this was something that existed even 20 years ago, but I kinda thought it was little more than an urban legend back then. Something to joke about but took it about as seriously as looking for Bigfoot. Oh, how the past 5 years have opened my eyes. Legitimately at least half of the women I have gone out with have told me that at some point they have either been swingers, been in an open marriage, considered themselves poly, or used to go to sex parties. Without exception they have all told me that is does not work. Given, it did not work out for them so their perception will be different than people who have managed to make it work for years. The stories they have told me and how much damage it has done to them is a warning to all which is be careful. Good rule of thumb, if you are having a hard time making one work, two or three probably isn't the answer.

On the topic of open marriages… If you start out this way and you both agree to it, I have known some people who have made this work-ish. Rare, but possible. Definitely takes a certain sort. From dating plenty of women who have been involved in this at one point or another, I can tell you without question that if this is brought up years down the line you just need to end the relationship and save yourself all the drama and heartache. If the guy brings it up, he will soon realize she can get a whole lot more dick than he ever dreamed of getting pussy and she should drop him on the grounds of being profoundly stupid. If she brings it up, 100% chance she already has her plan in motion and she is just looking for retroactive permission. Either way, it is a death sentence for the relationship.

A little over two years ago I was fishing in a bass tournament at Grand Lake. What shocked me was NOT the fishing (it was okay). It was all the giant ocean going vessels on that lake. Many of them had a dozen late teens and early 20's semi naked chicks prancing around with a couple late 40's and 50's looking dudes. Those girls did nothing to get on that boat but to look pretty and be willing to screw everything in sight. All those men did was work for 20 years and earn enough money to be able to afford a 3 million dollar boat and provide these girls with a couple day lifestyle they've seen on Instagram. The debate about men are naturally builders and women are naturally consumers ended that weekend for me. It was on full display for that whole weekend. Considering I'd guess most of those guys have kids older than the girls I saw on board I would question their moral compass a bit, but then again it is their life to live and their consequences to bare.

On a vaguely similar note, one of my friends told me about how she financed a Chevy Impala years ago. Guess she was a little low on money so the car salesman informed her that she, "had a pretty mouth," and that he'd cover her down payment for a blow job on the spot. Anyone else hearing a Banjo? Anyhow, she agreed to a blow job for him to pay the $1500 down payment. 2 minutes later and $1500 down the pipe. One of those moments if a desk could talk, oh the stories they would tell. The impressive part to her was the covert tattoo he has on his dick. So, ladies, if you're looking to get a free downpayment and have a pretty mouth just look for the covert-dicked car salesman. It'll be over before you know it. Suppose he actually paid the $1500 or just used a factory rebate and creative financing behind the scenes?

To the car salesman, the part time lawn mower in town who offered a discount to a semi-disabled girl, and all the other pieces of shit out there… I do not care if you feel like you're doing them a favor and some how you're justifying that behavior. I don't even care that she may be perfectly happy to blow you for a downpayment on a car. You are intentionally damaging another human being who often is in a situation where they feel desperate and hopeless. You are preying upon that desperation. You are taking perhaps the most intimate act a woman can perform on a man, and shitting all over it without regard for anyone else. I'm lumping you in as a sexual predator. Your victim may be perfectly fine with it, or they may go to their step father completely destroyed and tell him what happened – either way – I hope the Earth opens up and swallows you - good riddance.

Which brings me to an important topic which we have discussed a bit, but we need to dig in deeper. People who think they are worth far more in the dating and relationship marketplace than they actually are. Just in looks alone, so many women claim to be 10's when it is obvious they are far from it. In my 42 years I have known one legit 10. She maintained that level for about 5 years. She is still a real-deal 8 a solid decade past her prime and will be one of those women who could pass for a hot 47 year old when she is 60. Even at 60 though an average 22 year old girl will have all the cards in the dating scene. Nothing turns a man off faster than an entitled, bitter, angry woman who has an axe to grind and an unrealistic perception of herself. If we're playing the 1 to 10 game, here is a cheat code for you ladies. If you're actually a 6 and someone asks you what you rate yourself, don't get mad. Just say, "I am probably a 5 with some good days," then smile and be kind. Right there on the spot that man will consider you an 8 in the looks department and a 10 in the emotional department because you accurately self reflected and remained calm when so very few can. I do not know a single man who'd rather be with a bitter, insane 9 than a down to earth, kind 5. NONE.

For the guys, your looks just like hers will only last for so long. You can prolong this with how you take care of yourself, but on a long enough timeline we all end up old followed pretty quickly by dead. Just remember, your looks only last so long, but being an asshole is forever. One day you will not have the luxury of being an arrogant asshole. Facts do not care about your feelings either. Your value is not in how you look, so stop trying to be something you're not. Here is a little cheat code for you… women are attracted to assholes but rarely keep them forever. Being an asshole makes the odds of you being financially successful higher. So, when she gets tired of your BS she will divorce you and take a heavy half plus payments. Strong and stable is good – standing up for yourself and having convictions is good – NOT being humble and hiding your insecurities through being an asshole guarantees no one will miss you when you're dead (especially her). Food for thought…

This brings me to another point for both men and women to pay attention to. Do not rush into being too serious too quickly because it takes years to really get to know someone. It will take years to really know their family and friends too. To get to know their habits. To see how they react to positive and negative situations. To see how they react to mistakes and how they accept consequences. To see if they are manipulative or genuine. To learn about their history. You'd be shocked how many women have been on those boats and what they did to stay on them. You'd be shocked to know how many men used to be drug dealers and have a criminal history. You'd be shocked to know how many women have engaged in swinger lifestyles, cum shot parties, and orgies. You'd be shocked to know how many men put on a show of being wealthy when in fact it is all little more than a mirage. Be careful when it comes to moving in together too because in some states that can become common law pretty quick. Before you know it there can be legal ramifications heading your way if the relationship turns south. As my grandmother used to tell me, "Patience is the greatest virtue." Know who you are committing to before actually committing.

Gentleman… rarely should you believe a woman's tears. Unless you see a bone sticking out of her skin, blood gushing out of her body, or she just found out a close family member died those tears are not to be trusted or allowed to influence your choices. If it doesn't make any sense for her to be crying don't buy the BS. These tears are turned on and off at will and can be used as a manipulation tactic to get you to cave in or feel bad for her poor choices and lack of accountability. I have personally seen full on blabber mouth, speaking in tongues, loss of motor functions, crying with snot and tears flowing - only for it to stop instantly the moment they realized it was not going to work. Also, be warned that once the tear strategy fails it is almost always followed by anger. If you see this scenario unfolding get out your phone and start recording or make sure to have witnesses to the freak show. The reason for this is quite often what follows anger are accusations that you then have to defend against. Without a witness or proof that you are being framed there is a real chance that you'll have an uphill battle defending yourself in the world we live in today. Once the tears start that is your que to either get the phone out and start recording, make sure you have witnesses who are impartial, or get out of that situation and be somewhere else.

Also… gentleman, _NEVER_ cry in front of your woman, ever, unless there is a valid reason for it. Unless you have a bone sticking out of your skin, blood gushing out of your body, or you just found out a close family member died those tears will make her question the level of respect she has for you and will influence her choices. Crying is not going to solve your problems. Crying will only create more problems for you and make others around you question your authority to lead because down deep all women know tears can be tools for manipulation and pity. Weak men get cheated on because they act like women – no woman wants to be manipulated or have a pity party for a person they're supposed to count on. No woman wants to get on her knees for a man whom they believe to be weaker than they are. If you are choosing to cry in front of your wife or girlfriend without a solid reason you are inviting her to question your strength of will and clarity of mind. You are making a choice to plant the seed of doubt in her mind that you are not qualified to lead and that she can do better. Even more so, many women will punish you for this weakness. They will use your weakness as an invitation to pile on even more bad behavior. Like I said before, weak men create cruel women. Women respect strength and the ability to deal with problems and solve them without complaint. Crying all the time to get your way is about as counter-productive to a healthy relationship as you can get. No one likes a weak, sobbing mess – so don't do it! Here's a cheat code for you… Get over it and go have some fun together and avoid dwelling on depressing BS.

Side note… If you really have mental and emotional problems, please get help from people who won't use your problems against you or lose respect for you because of your struggles. You are not alone I assure you. People are stronger as a group than isolated individuals. Find that support system and don't give up!

The modern woman's formula for problem resolution is… Deflect, avoid, being passive aggressive, gaslight, crying, anger, accusations, attempts at personal insults, temper tantrum, vindictive behavior, beg for a 2nd chance, repeat. Guys… RUN!!!!!! She is not to be trusted. This kind of woman will intentionally harm you long before she will hold herself accountable. Bad enough to be around this kind – don't you dare have children with her too. This is the recipe for suicide in a man if he gets too invested and she uses that investment against him.

I'd give you the modern man's formula for problem resolution, but it is the exact same. Just add a dash of misplaced pride and bragging somewhere and it's ready to serve. Ladies… RUN!!!!!!!! Run as fast as you can! This kind of man isn't a man at all. He's a counterfeit man with all the parts on the outside but the insides are all twisted up.

Here's a cheat code for you guys… It's far more important for a woman to respect you than it is to like you. Being likable and having a fun personality sure helps. But there are plenty of great guys who are likable and sweet that will never have success in a relationship if they stay that way because being likable doesn't help her respect you at all (often it is counter-productive). There are plenty of assholes who operate on pursuing their own goals in life who earn the respect of their woman and in turn she gives them everything even though as a person she doesn't really care for him. She respects him because she believes long term he can protect and support her lifestyle through leadership that she trusts. Best place you can be is somewhere in the middle, but if in doubt be less likable and more focused on your goals and odds are you'll notice outcomes getting better for everyone involved. Remember, a good woman does everything for your success. A terrible woman does everything for her success.

Here's a cheat code for you ladies… It is not difficult to attract a man, but to retain them takes sustained reciprocation and effort. If you want to retain him here is the super-duper recipe with cherries on top. First, be loyal and do not hide reality from him about your past or what your intentions are about his future. This creates trust and accountability both ways. Second, always be respectful to him so long as he is doing the things he should be pursuing. If he is grinding away in pursuit of those goals you need to let him know how much you appreciate those efforts and successes for you and reward him for it constantly (as in daily) without games or manipulation. Lastly, when you two are out together you need to make everyone that sees you two together wonder how on Earth he got that lucky and what is he doing to make you that in love with him. That sustained effort has to come from you. You do that and odds are you'll keep him forever. No man should ever settle for less. Give him the best deal imaginable and odds are he'll take it.

Which brings up the next point that is it's FAR better to be single than in the wrong relationship. Most people I know (including myself) are not in a place to sustain a meaningful, committed relationship. It doesn't help that there are so few viable options, but that is the world we live in now. People make it work and sludge through one misery after another, but it's just painful to watch let alone be a part of. It doesn't help that quite often people never really take much time from one person to the next, and then add in the reality which is most of us are attracted to people who are all wrong for us -- you end up with constant train wrecks, broken homes, betrayal, drama, suicide, bankruptcy, single parents with children that grow up thinking this is okay, etc. If you find yourself in this cycle, try being single for a while. Take a deep breathe. Get back on your grind and pursue your goals without distractions or black holes for your emotions and time. If you aren't ready for something real and the person you are considering is all wrong for you (remember the math problem at the very beginning) even though you think everything is great, odds are your outcome will be far different than you expected and not for the better. Bogus values give way to bogus solutions.

For both men and women, be careful who you let into your life and even more careful whom you give second chances to. Don't concern yourself with losing them if they're already forming an exit strategy or did so long ago. Remember earlier I said the person with the most emotional investment gets the scraps – they are counting on this and often are enjoying your agony. You already lost them. Move on. Don't ever chase them. Don't take out your frustrations and anger on the innocent. Don't stop your pursuit of goals and remember the best revenge is quiet success and earned self-respect. Don't be surprised if years down the road they come back wanting that second chance. If they weren't loyal enough in the hard times, they don't deserve you in the good times.

Speaking of train wrecks… Want to know how to create a, "modern Feminist?" The ideal recipe starts with a school system that confuses their identity and replaces their innocence with a dark ideology. Throw in a couple bad influences like damaged friends and drugs. Then add a single parent who doesn't set boundaries and just hands them internet access because that is easier than actual parenting. That computer or phone is instant access to social media and dating apps. Social media is a mirage that confuses her even more and sets unrealistic expectations which in turn inflates her perceived self-worth OR diminishes it drastically because she is now comparing herself to things that do not even exist in the first place. Dating apps benefit a hand full of guys and give the vast majority of women an even greater false sense of value. The end result is these women are hooking up with the same handful of men. These men have no interest in commitment, and why would they? Most of these women aren't worth committing to by the time they've reached this point and these men got to that level by focusing on themselves and that is what made them attractive in the first place or they are so genetically gifted they have no incentive to try harder. So, when these women have their highest value in the dating market (late teens through her mid 20's) they're out getting plowed by guys who have no interest in reciprocating any value. After 80 dudes have obliterated every hole she's got and added layer upon layer of self volunteered trauma she eventually has enough (kinda). By this point though she is imprinted by this type of man. She will always lust for that guy who treats her terribly even though she will claim the opposite. That trauma is so engrained by her late 20's that she begins to act like and look like the very thing she claims to hate. She'll have a roster of at least 5 guys, thus making it all the more difficult for her to bond with one. She'll keep a hand full of orbiters and nice guys around for attention and free food but under no circumstances would she consider being with them. They are way too predictable, stable, and caring. She'll have a couple studs who get to use her as a receptacle for nothing in return, all fueled by the free food from the date she just got done with by the nice guy. This goes on for a few years. It seems healthier and more rewarding than her high school and college gang bangs and sex parties, but in reality, is cementing her inability to ever bond with someone who isn't unstable and abusive. All the sudden she is mid 30's and the looks are starting to fade. That is when she has the, "oh shit," moment and realizes she needs to cash in the chips she has left because her value is going down while the cartoon character she now needs to rope in is on his way up. Now it is time to find a retirement plan in the form of a sucker who will accept a bad deal with misrepresented information. One of those orbiters or a nice guy. Time to switch from Tinder and Adult Friend Finder and hop on Match and Bumble because she is done with the hot girl decade and a half. She has to find someone who will accept bare minimums across the board but is expected to give maximums in return. She will never let him do to her for everything he's got what she let so many in her past do for free or even paid for herself. It is time to balance the equation in her mind. Time to get back at the patriarchy. Time to give the least amount possible for the greatest amount in return because she's empowered now. This poor bastard gets to pay above new car prices for a ride missing both airbags, two kids in the back with neither father in sight, smells like rotten fruit, couple rolls of crime scene tape in the trunk, faulty sensors, with 450k hard miles and a stretched-out seat.

The, "strong and independent," modern feminists are pulling their blue and pink hair out after reading that. Don't blame me though, that is just a composite of the past 5 years of experiences I have had and what I have seen others deal with. Men, these kinds of women are to be avoided at all costs (this is priority one). They expect a traditional role from you without a backbone but have no intention of giving you anything traditional in return, honesty about their past, or intentions about your future. They might have a vagina and some of them don't look like men yet, but without exception they all end up looking and acting like the very thing they hate – and that is the guy they secretly lust for (and that aint you). And now you get to pay the price for a past you didn't create. You do not want to be on that ship when it goes down. Don't try to tread water where so many other men have drowned.

On that note, I guess it is time for me to list the 5 kinds of women whom you as men need to avoid like the Black Plague.

1. If she self describes herself as a baddie, a Queen, boss bitch, empowered, strong, independent, strong and independent, a modern feminist, an extreme feminist, rants about the patriarchy, or in general hates men across the board because of situations from their past - you need to get to the life

boats immediately. These types are profoundly conditioned and damaged. Remember, her past is a great guide to what your future will be. In time, these kinds of women will become what they claim to hate. They will also expect you to give up your pursuits and will power, but will then turn around and hold that choice against you. A side note to this kind is most of these ladies have terrible money management skills and loads of debt to support their fantasy lifestyle. Remember, once you put a ring on it, her debts become your debts while your money becomes her money. They're only strong and independent when it suits their needs.

2. If she has a bunch of meaningless tattoos, colored hair, long nails, excessive make up, random piercings, are pro-abortion and pro-trans yet claims to be a feminist you need to never even step foot on the Titanic in the first place. These are the kind that talk about, "manifesting," outcomes – so my advice is manifest a new girlfriend. Or God forbid they start talking about your sign and some astrological nonsense, just refer to the 8-sided red thing at the corner and remember not to turn down her street ever again. Add in an abuser, two convicts, and three drug dealer ex's and you have the recipe for a self-imposed disaster. Unlike the boss bitch who at least is trying to have some self-respect, this type of woman embraces self destructive behaviors and has no self-esteem. They are controlled by their emotions and fantasies, and even more dangerous is they have a tendency to make long term choices based on these short term feelings. In time, these are the ones who end up being dreadful to be around who adopt the true RBF (resting bitch face). Society calls them, "Karens," but I'm sure that doesn't seem great for women named Karen who are actually kind and operate in reality. Perhaps calling them, "future recruits to the RBF army," would be a more reasonable title for these creatures. If they are unable to treat themselves well, why should you expect them to treat you any better in the long run?

3. If she keeps you in the friend zone there is a reason why. That why is she only likes the attention and resources you provide for her with no reciprocation of value required. Does that sound like a good deal to you? These kinds of women love having a bunch of orbiters to get food, entertainment, and emotional support from. These are the same women who have a couple men who come around to blow out their bowels for free. Good rule of thumb guys – rules are only meant for the men she does NOT want. Women do not negotiate real attraction. If it feels off or you're jumping through hoops that is because she is making it difficult for you. These kinds of women love to waste your time and resources and know you're too weak and foolish to complain (don't be naïve, they think it is hilarious too). For the men whom they respect, there are no rules and there is no waiting. These men do not have to provide any resources and do not have to put up with any time wasting because she is the one pursuing them. Which man do you want to be? Do you really want to be either?

4. If she is selling her image online or posting semi naked pictures of herself on social media or porn sites, she is nothing more than a digital prostitute. Her value is only as much as the lowest price necessary to see her naked. Have no pity for this kind of woman because she is the one who set her own value. Just as ridiculous, this kind of woman will always feel like they have no use for men and make fun of them for being so desperate that they pay to see pictures of them – yet these weak guys are the ones who are financing their lives. Online is forever and she is trying to solve temporary problems involving drugs, past trauma, emotional damage, and money issues with permanent solutions that will create even more problems later on. A woman's value is in large part her sexual scarcity – and she is selling her value online for random strangers to jerk off to. It is no different than an economics model and these kinds of women treat it as such so you should too. These are not the kind

of problems you want to invite into your life. Want your dad or a coworker to find her college sex tape online or her Only Fans account? Is that reeeaaaalllly what you want to talk about in front of a board of execs at your work when an opportunity comes up for promotion? That what you want your future kids to have to deal with at school 17 years from now? Just imagine for a moment what sophomore year is like when all your classmates have seen your mom get dismantled by two dudes at once. There are plenty of good women out there with way less land mines and baggage to avoid later in life, so be picky and don't rush into an epically poor choice.

5. The woman who does not take care of herself physically. Very few men want to be with a woman who outweighs them by 75 pounds. A little extra can be a lot of fun, but there comes a point where it goes from curves to bulges – that's a line to consider before even thinking about commitment. For the vast majority, being morbidly obese is a chronic choice. I always find it funny when I see a video of a 350-pound woman saying she needs a man with a 10-inch cock… I wish I was in the background saying, "yeah, because most of that length is wasted just trying to reach paydirt." It's like the electric car circus where 66% of the energy is wasted before it gets to the consumer. Hell, an average man never gets there at all. Imagine being that guy who's swinging 5.5 inches of glory – having to shove those legs up around her shoulders just to even see where he needs to go. That is just not an acceptable situation guys. Incline dumbbell presses should be left in the gym. If she hates herself enough to get that way and stay that way, why should you expect her to treat you any differently long term. Misery loves others to be miserable with them, and if you think it's difficult now just wait til she's older and riddled with massive health issues and is so far gone she can't turn it around. The point of no return often comes silently and long before people want to believe. That really what you want to have to deal with?

Before I give advice on these 5 kinds of women, I want you to know I am ABSOLUTELY fat shaming people who've let themselves go so far they do not hardly recognize themselves in the mirror anymore. Shame is a good thing when used constructively. Shame is the proper response when you've wronged someone else. In this case if this is you, that person you've wronged is yourself and those around you. You should feel bad for letting yourself go and making others have to deal with it. You should feel terrible for the 5 year old version of yourself that had all those dreams and now you can't fulfill them because you get stuck in doorways and on toilets. Let me guess – something bad happened in your past, right? So, your solution is to create a prison within your own body? I really do get it. I've had weight struggles at times in my life. In 6th grade I was 5' tall and had a 42-inch waist. If I didn't keep my diet and exercise in check, I would be one of those 350-pound guys using a motorized wheelchair at the grocery store. I'm done enabling you. I'm done saying it's okay. I do not want you to commit a multi decade suicide with food. I care enough about you to say stop killing yourself. I care enough about you to tell you the truth. Please get help. I'm not asking you to become an Olympic athlete who has 8% body fat. But I am asking you to ask yourself hard questions and start making some changes now that will save your life later. Please do the work to pursue those dreams you used to have. It is not too late UNTIL it's too late. If you don't start right now odds are you never will. Real empowerment starts by admitting most of us cannot do it all on our own. That doesn't mean it will be easy. But I can assure you having fissures in your ass with mold and bugs growing between your skin folds is far harder. If you had something traumatic in your past and your coping mechanism is eating, consider this – they want you to die of shame and guilt. They want you to be miserable. Prove them wrong and show them you aren't a voluntary victim. You are the one that has to take that first step. It's the hardest one but I believe in you.

My advice for these 5 groups of ladies is pretty simple. For group 1, do you really want to become the man who you let damage you? Do you want to impose that baggage on the next man in your life or your kids? Do you really want to try and compete at home after having competed in the work place all day? You're well on your way to being alone. Is that what you want? For your sake and those in your life I truly hope you ask yourself these questions and reflect on what got you to this point.

For group number 2, until you decide to operate in reality and make decisions based on facts instead of feelings, you'll never have stability and there is little point in going further with you until that point. One question to ask yourself… currently, do you even want stability? Many of you thrive on drama. This is why you tend to not like other women either. You thrive on it, are attracted to it, yet most will say they hate it. Bogus values give way to Bogus solutions.

For group 3, consider the saying what goes around really does go around. Right now, you attract all these men and for most of them you waste their time, soak up their attention, and use them for money and entertainment. You think it is funny. And I get it – they're suckers for falling for it. But, that lack of empathy and honesty will return to you many times over later in life. Those same men that you use and make fun of now will one day be the same ones that do that to you OR ignore you all together, mark my words. The one big difference between you and all those weak men is that they are used to rejection and you aren't.

For group 4, I get it. I have an acquaintance in town who years prior was an escort. She has told me she's been paid as much as 3k for half an hour's time. Now she makes less than $15 an hour for a job she hates. She has openly told me she will never be in a serious relationship ever again and is incapable of bonding. I have no idea if her image or videos of her exist online, but I cannot comprehend how difficult it will be for those around her one day. Please consider this before squandering your beauty and value for an easy buck at the expense of the rest of your life and those who care for you.

For group 5, there is another thing to consider. In my opinion, if years into a relationship you decide to let yourself go and become a morbidly obese woman that is a form of abandonment. Same can be said for a man if he does that too. Not just sexually, and not just the future burdens you are imposing on your family, but your image is a reflection of him just as he is of you. You are telling the world and his peer group that he is only worth a blob and he is willing to accept this. It is much easier to stay healthy than it is to get unhealthy and then try to reel it back in. None of this matters at all if you're bed ridden and helpless.

There are a few other kinds of women whom you need to look out for but may still be a quality enough to consider for an actual committed relationship. The first one is the kind that spend a lot of time on her phone and is very active on social media. This by itself isn't necessarily a bad thing. Some use this as a means of staying connected to a large friend group and some use it for a stream of income. The dangers here are who is in that friend group and are they using their social media as a jumping board into digital prostitution? I have news for you – all women have secrets they do not want you to know. If they guard their phone like a hawk then they have things in their life you do not want to be a part of. Often when people (men and women) stay plugged in too long they lose the ability to apologize for their mistakes or accept consequences for their actions. Remember, people become a composite of whom they spend their time with. If they spend all their time with a computer, they will become a computer. Simultaneously, they lose the ability to appreciate the good things in their lives and the efforts others make for them. This is more than a red flag – it's red alert. Watch for co-dependency traps and if they go out of their way to sabotage your life to feel better about their own. Just please be careful and stay aware.

Single mothers… Be VERY careful. I have met a couple single mothers who were really good people who had escaped from bad situations. I have met a couple who are widowed. Without exception they all have baggage. We all do, but their baggage is different. They have children from another man or multiple men. Most of them helped create situations where either the man decided to leave or they decided to leave him, even with children involved. For a lot of them, the moment that father or a flame from years past comes back they will drop you for that guy because they were never really over him no matter how bad he was and she is imprinted to that kind of guy now. I've never fully understood why trauma creates imprinting, but it is undeniable that with trauma comes imprinting in single moms. Case in point, the woman who I miss the most and had the best chemistry with is now re-married to a guy she'd been married to previously. She is not happy with him, but can't get away from his traps. Even if she has it together and is a great person, you need to know going in that you will never be a priority in her life compared to those kids. You are volunteering to be a part of a group project with those kids. You need to be aware that she can take those children from you and there is nothing you can do about it even if you dedicated years to fathering another man's children. You will have the responsibilities of being a father without the authority of a father when it boils down to it. You need to ask yourself why she had a child with that guy or guys, but could not retain that man or those men long term even with the responsibilities they created?

High maintenance and drama queens… Just like the player, you know what you're getting yourself into with this kind. I have no pity for you as a man if you decide to go this route just like the woman who decides to pursue the player. This is the hot/crazy scale moment. You better make sure it's worth it, because even if it is there are real costs involved. If you decide to engage in this kind of woman, do not complain to me after the fact that she took you to the cleaners and then screwed all your friends for fun just to make you nuts. The moment you show weakness to this kind of woman your replacement is already in the pipeline. You are warned.

Going back to phone addiction and excessive social media utilization… This ends up damaging a person's ability to communicate effectively, let alone bond. Women have always had a level of expectation that guys are supposed to read their minds, but now with all this social media influence they expect you to not only read their mind but be able to provide a fantasy that they have seen on someone else's Instagram that doesn't even exist in the first place. Both men and women have the problem of saying one thing but wanting another in relationships (been there, done that). But of all thing's men are good at, reading minds and decoding fantasies is something none of us can do well. Be direct and state your intentions and men will respond well to this even if they don't want the same things. Men, ask for what you want and at least have the common courtesy to reciprocate the directness (women like direct, fyi).

Online dating is so funny to me. I've tried it on and off. It is great for comedy relief because some of the pictures, profile names, and summaries are so stereotypically ridiculous that even if you never get anywhere with it at least you can say it was incredible comedy. For the guys, don't get mad if they don't respond to you. Most of them are just there for the attention from the top few percent of men. A lot of them are married and either looking for an outright affair or looking for some insane poly hexagon cluster hive. Plus, a lot of the profiles aren't even real – they're either creations from the dating service or scammers trying to steal your identity. Either way, it's not really dating anyhow. The past couple years my profile summaries would just be a list of outrageous failed dates I'd been on and the insane things that happened on them. For the ladies, realize that those handful of guys that you really want are being pursued by all the women. He may sleep with you a few times, but he is not going to commit to you unless you are truly on his level across the board and willing to give him such an unbelievable long term deal that he can't refuse. If you keep getting the same results, change a variable. I looked up synonyms for online and on the list was, "ready for use," which I think perfectly summaries online dating. Everyone scrambling for the most benefits for the least amount in return possible.

Even more ridiculous are the married people who are pursuing affairs behind their spouse's backs. Anyone remember the whole Ashley Madison debacle? You cannot find an exact number of profiles that got hacked, but for sure it was over 32 million. 32 MILLION! WTF is wrong with people. That is a legit percentage of the total number of married people. I get it, some were one time users. Some profiles were fake to entice suckers into thinking there were more options than there really were. But most were real, and will be low hanging fruit forever and ever. All these dating platforms, social media, and porno sites are primed for digital extortion in the future.

I've touched on this subject earlier, and I think it is worth mentioning again. If you're in a committed relationship with an expectation of monogamy and you just cannot control yourself when it comes to the temptations and opportunities to cheat it's time to be single. Save everyone including yourself a whole lot of heartache and drama and just be honest about your intentions before being disloyal to whomever you're with. Most people don't like overwhelming drama and almost everyone values loyalty. A big part of being loyal is founded on honesty. Even if your partner doesn't like what they are hearing, without question they'd rather at least be given the respect of honesty before making a move than finding out down the line about what went down without a chance for themselves to decide what they need to do. Kinda a Golden Rule moment – treat others as you'd wish to be treated.

So, who likes a good story?

1. The last actual date I went on started out well. We walked and talked for a couple hours and the conversation was all over the board. We get back to the vehicles and just keep talking. Then, she brings up the idea that I could come over some time and watch her get plowed by some other dude. I laughed for so long I think she was getting mad. Needless to say, we did not meet again.

2. I met a really nice lady at a restaurant. She was the real deal in the looks department. Great conversation, eye contact, could feel the sparks, etc. Right as dinner was ending she informed me that we needed to go back to my place and spend the night together. I was not necessarily opposed to this, but I had a couple questions for her. The first question I asked was, "what is my name?" Now, for context, we'd been chatting online for over a week and she'd written my name a bunch of times and we'd talked on the phone prior to the date and she knew my name. And… She had no idea what my name was. There was no need to ask anymore questions. I very politely and calmly told her that I couldn't sleep with her. Her reaction to that was rage. It was wild. The date was done. Looking back, I think I was the first person who'd ever told her no. That was the moment I realized rejection, even if it is warranted, is nearly impos-

sible for some women to handle. To this day I think of her a couple times a week. So many valuable lessons all within that hour.

3. I met another lady at a restaurant, and again we were having a great time. Solid eye contact, good conversation, etc. About 20 minutes into it she tells me she knocked out her last husband and they both got arrested. My gut says he probably deserved it. But damn, can't that wait for pillow talk a couple months down the line? Ended up being a good woman whom I still care about, but that moment was the reason why I would not have committed to her.

4. Met yet another lady at a restaurant (I think restaurants may be out come to think of it). This one felt odd from the start. Before the meal even hit the table, she exclaimed to me that she was, and I quote, an, "extreme feminist," and proceeds to start in on her Extreme Feminist Manifesto (an EFM). I sat and listened for a solid 10 minutes just absorbing her rant. After she ran out of steam, I very calmly told her that, "I love women too." Turns out, that might not be the brightest thing to say to an, "Extreme Feminist." Finally, the tab comes and I go to pay the bill. That is when she starts to lose it because I was going to buy her meal. I looked right at her and said, "I'm not buying you a Lambo, just an $8 burger." The debate on whether you should EVER date a modern feminist is over.

5. This one is special. We intended to go to a restaurant for an actual meal, but we never made it. I go to pick her up at her folks' place (not judging – hell, I'd want to live in that pad too). We're heading to the restaurant and right as we are getting into town she asks if I can pull into Walmart. Kinda odd, but I say sure. By the time we get inside I can hear the Twilight zone theme playing softly in the background. For perspective, the previous several days she had told me how much she was into diet, fitness, exercise, etc – all things I have always found very attractive. She looked the part too back then. She proceeds to pick up a giant

Lunchable (didn't even know they made a legit tray size), 1 pound bag of jelly beans, a big bag of beef jerky, and a 1 liter of cheap orange pop. We get to the checkout line and I watched her spend $17 on that crap. I bought myself a bottle of water. Our plan for fajitas on me was out the door. I took her back to her folk's place. By this point any notion of serious commitment was gone, but I am WAY too curious to let this happen without watching. We go inside and sit in this kitchen with a cool island table and I watched her consume all of it over the course of about 45 minutes. I had no idea a 135 pound woman could do what I had just witnessed. The best descriptive I would compare it to would be engulfed. Her folks were 20 feet away watching TV acting like this was just standard operating procedure. I knew she had gone through a lot. She is not a bad person. BUT… this is such a valuable learning experience that it needs shared with you. Ladies, don't claim to be something you are not. Guys, don't cause so much trauma in her life that she cannot handle even getting some Mexican food without having to cope with 5 pounds of nuclear waste when interacting with the next guy. As a whole, we can and should be better.

6. Turns out referrals can be dangerous too… Thanks to rave reviews at a local office, I'm adding this one in. A friend of mine tells me I really need to meet this lady. So, I agree to it and we go out. The date goes great. It was a real date. Picked her up, go on an actual date, then dropped her back off. We agreed to meet a couple days later and go on a 2nd date. The night of the 2nd date comes and I'm literally 5 minutes from leaving to go pick her up and I get a text. The text reads something along the lines of sorry for the late notice but I can't make it tonight. I get it – life happens. Then less than a minute later I get a second text. It read, and I quote, "Let yourself in, I'm in the shower." Sometimes those accidental texts meant for someone else can be real gems.

Going in and paying my bill today was the best thing that has happened to me all week. I had an opportunity to speak with 4 people who've all been in long term marriages. I had an opportunity to speak to four people who still believe in monogamy and til death do us part. Refreshing perspectives that I needed to hear. They have little clue what it is really like out there in the, "dating," market and I'm thankful. I'm thankful that there is still innocence even in adults. I'm thankful for their ignorance. I'm thankful that there are people who understand accountability that don't know the sour taste of betrayal. Loyalty in real time is the greatest sign of respect. To the four of you, thank you for showing me your reality in motion and giving me hope that sustained bonds still exist. You are beautiful to me.

Here is another huge topic we need to discuss. Prenuptials… I have good news and I have bad news. We'll start with the bad news first. Marriage is now a contract between you and the government. You may have heard something about God in the vows, but he's just kicking it with the Aliens to watch the circus from above. The good news is ALL of you already have a prenuptial agreement in place if you're married. The only question is did you write it or did the government write it for you? Of all the people to be asking for pre-nuptials, women should be on the front lines because most of the time they have the most to lose and the most to gain from divorce. And refer back to the beginning – do you really want to be on that airplane without your own parachute? Or would you rather lawyers and a court system from decades ago provide you with a generic one that was packed by people who may not have your or your children's best interests at heart? For the men, this is an absolute no brainer. Divorce is expensive and odds are your plane is going to crash. Blind faith in another human who is incentivized to leave you at some point is not a great strategy for life long blissful marriage. Until the system de-incentivizes divorce, not having a prenuptial for everyone involved is absolute lunacy. For both men and women, stop co-mingling accounts and assets too because when you go to court it's a much steeper hill to climb than if you kept it all separate. For men and women both, refer back to Moral Hazard and take a few minutes to consider this concept before making any lifelong decisions.

The results are in, and paternity test should be mandatory before any man signs the birth certificate. There are millions of children in this country who have dad's that aren't really dad. Meaning there are millions of fathers that think those are their kids but in fact those are some other dude's kid. Once you sign that birth certificate, you're dad. Even if you find out years down the road that kid isn't yours you may still be legally responsible to pay for some other guy's spawn. Then you have to make hard choices whether you remain quiet and carry on as though nothing is wrong for the sake of the child or you can blow up the whole thing and then still potentially be on the hook.

A few questions you men need to consider before ever committing…

1. Was she doing things with other men before you that she is not willing to now do with you? (Acts, frequency, enthusiasm, initiation, etc)
2. Is she a net asset or a net liability to your future? (In other words, is she adding or subtracting from your future and making efforts to make your life better)
3. Is her WORST behavior something you're willing to deal with long term?
4. Is she trustworthy and respectful? (Her phone is a good start on knowing this answer)
5. Is she feminine by nature or masculine by nature?
6. When you treat her like a queen does she turn around and treat you like a peasant?
7. Is she loyal even though she has options? (They all have options by the by)
8. Is she in Love with you or in Love with the lifestyle she thinks you can provide her?
9. Does she encourage you to make the big decisions?
10. Does she laugh and smile or is she a grump with an axe to grind?

A Few Questions you women need to ask before ever committing…

1. Is this a man that is respected amongst his peers?
2. Is this a man that has a problem with wasting time or using time ineffectively?
3. Does this man control his emotions or do his emotions control him?
4. Is he accountable to his actions? (Accountable, in my opinion, is NOT making a bad choice even though you know you could have)
5. Does this man seem like he's trying to take short cuts in life and his career or is he long term goal oriented and willing to do things the right way?
6. Is he providing you enough attention, affection, and respect to quench your thirst for it so one day when times are tough you won't go looking for his replacement?
7. Does he call you out when you make a mistake and compliment you when you do well?
8. Is this a man you could see being willing and able to sacrifice himself to protect you and a future family together?
9. Is this a man who is confident enough in his decision making to make the tough calls without asking permission to do so?
10. Does he laugh and smile or is he a grump who's making the choice to be a chronic downer?

Rejection can be a very hard pill to swallow. As men, we face rejection and defeat on a regular basis whether we recognize it or not. The most successful men lose far more than they win even if they don't recognize it. Competition is in our nature and we can only reach our ceiling through competition and risk taking while embracing consequences both good and bad. This is a reality we should embrace without anger, jealousy, resentment, or fear because rejection is a wonderful teacher just like it's big brother (failure) if you allow it to be.

For women, rejection is much harder for them to accept because they operate through a Lense of emotions. This is why they rarely initiate interactions with men even if they want to. That fear of rejection over powers their desires more often than not. Most women are not meant to compete the same way men do long term. This is NOT a negative, it is just reality. Do not use this against them, but instead value that side of them and protect it. You want a woman's trust? Protect their weaknesses and genuinely compliment them when they succeed OR fail after taking on a risk and accepting the consequences without complaint.

Human nature tends to avoid all things negative consequence. Those consequences come after someone's accountability to options fail and they abandon their responsibilities. Even sociopaths and true narcissists understand this concept (and often will use it against you) even though they do not feel and experience reality the same way most people do. Accountability is NOT making a poor choice in the first place. If you want to avoid negative consequences, start by taking accountability seriously and be mindful of your weaknesses and vices so you don't get tempted in the first place. This is where having a group of true friends who will hold you accountable can make all the difference.

The past 5 years have proven to me (my truth) that the more sexual partners a person has had in their life, the more likely it is they'll not be able to bond with any one person. I have also seen a trend (my truth) that the more partners a woman has had in her past the more likely it is she will cheat. To a lesser extent I think this is also the case with men too. Men are wired differently, but the same patterns end up destroying them as well – it just looks different on the outside is all. Men start looking at women as little more than a receptacle once they've had too many partners. Women start looking at men as either monsters or a paycheck once they've had too many partners. Both sides end up being the same in that the more partners they have the more likely it is that they will disconnect the value of the person they are with versus what they can leverage from that person. These are my observations – use this experience to avoid problems, drama, being used, and unappreciated. If it doubt, take a step back and protect your mind and body before making a rushed choice with potentially long-term consequences.

As I see it, modern marriage is little more than a retirement plan for broken women who are trying to hedge against their depreciation and weak men who feel like they have no options and don't value themselves or their future's. The idea of a no-fault divorce is comedy to me – why not just call it encouraged Moral Hazard and be done with it. The incentivization of bad behavior, followed by financial incentives to break the contract and vows is a rigged game no one should play until the rules are changed. Don't get me wrong – the theory of marriage is a wonderful expression of commitment and team work to achieve common financial, reproductive, and emotional goals. But to enter into a system that encourages Moral Hazard is right back to the math problem at the beginning – bogus values give way to bogus solutions. Good rule of thumb… NEVER sign a contract where one or both parties are incentivized and even encouraged to break it.

For the men, here is a simple check list to refer to so you're staying focused on the things you need to do in relationship with a woman. (I'd say life in general too)

1. Are you using your time well or wasting it?
2) Are you avoiding addictions and vices that strip you of your potential and keeping other men in your life who help you stay accountable?
3) Are you taking your physical fitness seriously?
4) Are you keeping your emotions in check and not allowing anger or jealousy to control your words and actions?
5) Are you holding others responsible for their choices or are you enabling bad behaviors?
6) Are you praising others for their accomplishments and helping incentivize success in others around you?
7. Do you have the capacity to put other's needs ahead of your own?

For the women, here is a simple checklist to refer to so you're staying focused on the things you need to do in a relationship with a man. (I'd say life in general too)

1. Are you kind and respectful or are you combative and quick to anger?
2. Are you using your time wisely or wasting it?
3. Are you making rules and hurdles for your spouse or boyfriend? If so, you should ask yourself why…
4. Are you making him look good amongst his peers, family, and friends?
5. Are you making a conscious effort to be respectful and supportive of his goals and pursuits?
6. Are you taking your health and fitness seriously?
7. Are you spending too much energy on social media and communicating with people you know you should not be?

If he is providing resources, protection, masculine leadership, attention, the ability to solve problems, and is staying physically fit then in return she should be providing an easier home life, support for long term goals, great sex, kindness without drama, loyalty, and is staying physically fit too. If he is not providing that list, then why would she accept that? If she is not providing that list, then why would he accept that? More so, if he was providing this list at one point but is not anymore for no justifiable reason, then how is that not an abandonment of the relationship? If she was providing this list at one point but it not anymore for no justifiable reason, then how is that not an abandonment of the relationship? There is no excuse that justifies getting lazy and taking out that laziness on your spouse. As with most things in life, we only get what we pay for. ROI (return on investment) goes both ways.

Let me guess – this all sounds ridiculous to most of you… There is no way that's reality now days. There is no way that 20 years of unlimited access has changed reality to this point. Then again, no one would have believed Epstein Island existed until it was all over the news let alone all the other child brothels and storefronts being discovered. No one would have believed multiple governments would collude to create a virus that killed 7 million people for a social experiment to see how we'd react. From micro to macro, everything I have written is a reality now. It's not too late if we take a stand. Doing nothing is little more than just handing over the keys. It starts with each of us making a better choice today than we did yesterday and standing up for those who don't have a voice and saying no to bogus values.

For myself, I'm stepping away all together for however long it takes to get right for myself and wait until I find someone who is worth it. The second paragraph of this chapter sums it up for me – how is insanity working out there ole' Johnny boy? Repeating the same mistakes over and over again each time expecting a different result without changing any of the variables except the person in front of me. There is little need for relationships with no chance of commitment. It is more times than not pointless and counterproductive. For any satisfaction and relief that might be obtained, there is an equal or greater amount of shame and risk. There is no need to feel shame or being a part of the problem when looking back I have been just that at times. Just because someone means well that doesn't make everything okay. I've had multiple wake up calls. Perhaps it is time I pay attention to them. The society we live in now would say I've done little to nothing wrong. The women who I've seen for the most part would say I've done little to nothing wrong. But I know I have down deep. I am definitely not the hero of this story.

CHAPTER 4

Perspectives

The more I write the more I am realizing that our perspectives on reality and how accurately we understand facts and observable truths plays a huge part in our decision making processes. The further from reality our perspectives the more likely it is we will make insane and counterproductive choices. The closer our perspectives are to reality the more likely it is we will make sane and productive choices. Back to the very first paragraph in this book – bogus values give way to bogus solutions. The inverse is also true – accurate values give way to accurate solutions.

I really enjoy math, science, and having a broad range of knowledge. I think that knowing just how small I am helps me value my life that much more and see the beauty in this brief existence. This is a big reason why I regret the portions of my life where I have not used it wisely, because we only get so much time and once it's gone it is gone. The scarcity of my life is what makes it so valuable to me.

This past weekend I weighed in at 208 pounds. To the barn swallow that starred at me for a couple minutes that day, no doubt I was a giant. It was interesting to watch it watch me because I could tell it was scared of me, but curiosity overpowered its fear. To the Elephant I will see this Friday, I'm so inconsequential it won't even acknowledge my existence. Two very different perspectives of the same being. Now for a step further...

NASA says Earth is 7926 miles in diameter at the equator. To the Earth, that Elephant doesn't even qualify as small. I drive a lot, and even considering all I drive it takes me about 3 months to travel that far on average. But compared to our sun with a diameter of 865,370 miles, Earth is just a dot. Then consider how big our solar system is and things start to take on a whole new perspective. Even defining the size of our own solar system begins the process of estimating because it is so vast. Rather than measuring objects by miles, astronomers begin using AU's (Astronomical Units) to simplify distances. An AU is the average distance between Earth and the Sun (in miles, just shy of 93 million for simplicity). For scale, there are about 63,241 AU's in a Light year. A light year is the distance light travels in a vacuum for one year (roughly 5,879,000,000,000 miles, ballpark). The boundary of our solar system is widely considered the Oort cloud which is comprised of rocks and ice of varying sizes from dust particles to mountains. The diameter of this structure is an estimate which ranges from 2 to 6 light years. Even at this point, which in the scheme of things is sitting right next to us, it's little more than extrapolation.

Then consider our galaxy the Milky Way. Nasa says the Milky Way is roughly 100,000 light years across. Think about that for a minute. Our solar system is at a minimum 2 light years across and it'd take you almost 20 million years to travel across at highway speeds (12 trillion miles at 70 miles per hour). The Milky way is about 50,000 times further across. In other words, ballpark 1,000,000,000,000 years to travel across it at a highway speed of 70 miles per hour with no bathroom breaks.

This is where perspectives start getting really fun because from here on out we're little more than guessing because the size is so overwhelming and the distances involved are not really comprehendible. For instance, IC 1101 is a galaxy which may have as many as 100,000,000,000,000 stars and is a billion light years from us. Takes a long time for that light to get here so we can see what it looked like a billion years ago. It is so large that light from its furthest point takes millions of years longer to get here than its closest point to us. And that is just one, all be it incredibly large, galaxy in a sea of galaxies.

You ask how many galaxies? Depends on who you ask and when you ask… Current guesses range between 200,000,000,000 and 2,000,000,000,000 galaxies that we can see. In 20 years, this number may be a thousand times bigger or a hundred times smaller. This isn't exactly something any of us can really fact check with any rational expectation of accuracy. The size of this is so immense that it's a bit ridiculous to even try to comprehend except that with this absurdity comes perspective. The point isn't the exact number, it's the perspective.

Then calculate an estimated average of 100,000,000,000 stars per galaxy. Some people say it could be many times that – again, this is all speculation. Figure an average star has between one and ten planets, means Earth is far from alone. Even if you figure it as 1 planet per star, you're talking about a very conservative 100,000,000,000 planets times a very conservative 200,000,000,000 galaxies which means there is a very, very, very conservative 20,000,000,000,000,000,000,000 planets in just the universe that we can see.

It doesn't stop there because most of our universe we cannot see and we never will because it is moving away from us faster than the light it is emitting in our direction. Doesn't help that a lot of what's out there is literally invisible to us anyways. Nasa says we can see about 5% of the universe. My gut says that number was in part calculated based on a paper clipping drawn from a hat with the number 5 written on it. Light MAY have a speed limit, but space itself doesn't, and it's had billions of years to do whatever it wanted to. Four paragraphs above for me is what I would define as functionally infinite. What I'm talking about now is literally infinite and in fact could be infinite multiple times over and over and over again. Want to really blow your mind – read about objects over 40 billion light years away and how that's possible if the universe that we understand is less than 14 billion years old, but we can still see those objects yet can't see almost everything else.

That is about as far as my mind can go. No doubt there are people on this planet that can add another half a dozen paragraphs and poke holes in the paragraphs above if they try hard enough. That is not the point, although reading their perspectives would be very interesting. The point to that (besides the intrigue factor) is perspective. The barn swallow was only concerned about its survival when looking at me because I am 3000 times bigger than it is. The Elephant will automatically disregard me because I pose absolutely no threat to its survival from a physicality perspective because it is 75 times bigger than I am. I have no fear of the swallow and even if it dive bombed me, I doubt it'd even leave much of a bruise at the cost of its own life whereas the Elephant could crush me and not even know that it just killed me. The Earth is an amazing and truly huge place that we are so lucky to inhabit, yet it is not even one grain of sand on an immense beach. The broader our perspectives the more likely it is we will have a better understanding of our own lives and a better grasp of reality. The more we understand ourselves and the better grasp we have of reality the more likely it is we will make better decisions for the future. Accurate values give way to accurate solutions, and it starts with our own self-perception being on point.

My perspective was changed forever on 10-28-2018. Prior to that I'd only had a couple moments where things didn't quite add up, and there were outside chance explanations for what I'd seen. What happened at 4:05pm on 10-28-2018 has no outside chance explanations.

If you'd been 6 miles East of Ponca City, Oklahoma at 4:05pm on 10-28-2018 you'd have seen what we watched not long after passing the Sun N' Fun Park heading back towards town. If you'd looked up, you'd have first seen a light as bright as the sun but silver in color to the north of the sun. After a few seconds it stopped glowing and we could see the object. It was literally the size of a sky scrapper and it was levitating what I'd guess to be a mile up. It was smooth as far as I could tell with no wings, doors, windows, vents, engines, or seems. It was bright silver like polished steel and it was just levitating for a solid minute. And then like that with us staring at it the craft vanished. Mesmerized. Then Shazam! It was there, then it wasn't. It didn't fly away. It just disappeared instantly. The thing is right afterwards I looked around and saw two airplanes in line of sight and it happened on a perfectly clear day in a pretty well populated area. It was high enough in the sky that anyone in Ponca looking East would have seen it. Hard to miss a shiny object the size of the Sears tower just chilling out at 5000 feet.

That was the moment I knew we were not alone. I'd always figured we weren't alone. The universe is far too big and been around for far too long for us to be the only planet that went from geology to biology and managed to exist in that state long enough. But to see something like that which was clearly not man made gave me a valuable perspective. The perspective was how very small I am. The perspective was how very little I know. That perspective through experience has given me so much motivation to learn and to keep my eyes open because we never know when the next opportunity for gained perspective will happen. It could be a barn swallow. It could be a glowing red car sized object flying east above a city street. It could be failing a lift you think you should hit. It could be a glass sliding across a table on its own. It could be an attic fan starting up and the lights flickering on and off when talking about the paranormal with your brother. There is far more to this life than meets the eye.

A funny thing happened to me a few days after 10-28-2018 while lifting weights. Prior to this point, I'd never benched more than 275 for 2 reps and 225 for 11 reps. I'd stayed pretty level for about 15 years at that strength. A few dips and hills, but all in all that was where I'd been. Then just a couple days later I start my warm ups and something was very different. I go through my progression and I'm killing it. Get to 225 and I did 16 reps with it. I then threw on 275 and did it for 6 reps after having just done 5 reps more with 225 than I'd ever done in 23 years of lifting by that point. Within a couple weeks I was doing 275 for 8. And since then, that has become my new norm if I just rep out. Nothing else changed in my life. No anabolic steroid use or crazy supplements. No drastic dietary changes. I don't look any different. There are plenty of guys way stronger than me, but it is nice to have caught up a bit. One of those perspectives where you'll take what you can get. It's made it all the more clear to me that I need to cherish what I have because as we say, "one day on a long enough timeline the bar won't even move." The strength gain I experienced has made me appreciate what I have and made me all the more aware that one day even the bar will be too much.

Whether it was the experience that changed me, my mental perspective changing, or me letting go some stress in my life there was an obvious change in me that was measurable. It affected all my lifts that way. Shame the gains only lasted a couple weeks, but I am grateful for them sticking around. The only other noticeable change I have seen that continued was my eye sight. For the past several years my eye sight has improved and I am now 20/10 in both eyes at age 42. My focal point has moved out a bit, but my visual acuity has improved since 2018 when I was 20/15 or so. Odds are this change has nothing to do with what we saw, but it is something I have noticed since. To whoever was piloting that craft, thank you for the perspectives even though my gut says you weren't there for purely humanitarian reasons (felt more like a flex to me).

If you're bored some evening, I highly advise reading up on something called the Planetary Habitability Index. The idea behind this is to rank the known and observable planets and objects by the likelihood they can support life. It is truly fascinating to read about different star types, what a tidal lock is, the Goldie Locks zone, elements, the different kinds of planets, the potential for super habitable planets, mass to volume ratios, gravitation affects, atmosphere differences, volcanic activity, etc. Shout out to NASA, Big Think, and all the rest – it's really great stuff to consider even if some of it is extrapolation and theory. Over 5000 planets studied and quite a few are promising for life just out of that tiny sample. There is no way to know if there is life on them now or in the past because they are simply too far away to know for sure. However, several of the planets studied scored almost as well as Earth. That out of a relatively small sample size of 5000 and change.

The next logical question is how many planets out of 20,000,000,000,000,000,000,000 would be as suitable or even more suitable for life than Earth? Don't get me wrong, we won the cosmic lottery. If the odds are even as slim as 1 in a million planets are just as good or better than Earth that only takes 6 zeros off that number (which was a very conservative estimate in the first place). That is still a 2 with 16 zeros' after it if that is the case. Plus, you have to consider that is a snap shot of right now, not the past dozen plus billions of years that can be seen. Just because it doesn't support life now doesn't mean it wasn't a planet with thriving civilizations a billion years ago. And out of that 1 in a million, consider if 1 in a million of those have life as we understand it. That is still a 2 with 10 zeros. Say 1 in a thousand of those planets develop civilizations. Now it is 20,000,000. Say 1 in a 100 become interplanetary and/or intergalactic and manage to not kill themselves in the process. That means 200,000 intergalactic civilizations at this moment. Is all that total speculation – absolutely. A true statistician would say it's either 100% or 0%. Then again, that same statistician would also look at a sample size of a 2 with twenty-two zeros and say it's almost impossible for the number to be just one (Earth). What I can say with 100% certainty is the number is at least 2 (us and whoever made that craft).

Here is a perspective for you to consider on the wild speculation 200,000 is an accurate number. That sounds like a huge number. But is it? If there are between 200 billion and 2 trillion Galaxies in the universe we have the potential to see, but only 200,000 intergalactic civilizations to go around that means the vast majority of galaxies are void of any advanced civilization. We are a long way from this point, but it goes to show how lucky we really are to even consider the actual possibility we could get there one day. Truly the cosmic lottery winners – we bought the winning ticket; we're now just waiting for the numbers to be drawn. The danger is, what happens to most lottery winners? Most end up worse off after just a few years than if they'd not won at all. As a species we should keep that in mind.

I have spent almost 5 years reading about this subject matter. It has opened my mind to understanding and appreciating things far bigger than myself. It has also made me ask why would an advanced civilization capable of building the craft that I witnessed come here? Goes back a little to conflict theory where there is competition for resources. I can tell you with certainty we have no viable option to stop what I saw.

The past 9 months I've spent a great deal of time moving rocks to create fish habitat. The water level here is at least 6 feet low and I'm tired of fishing in water with no structure. But in lifting literally a million pounds of rock I have gained a different perspective through time under tension. I now know how difficult it is to pick up, walk with, and place a 2 cubic foot piece of lime stone. I am well fed and strong. Whenever I read or listen to some expert say that the Egyptians used slaves who were half my size that maybe ate a quarter what I do to move over 2 million stones weighing an average of 2.5 tons, with some stones weighing over 80 tons in literally perfect alignment I can't help but laugh at the absurdity of it. That being just one of the pyramids. I have an idea for the next Mel Brooks movie – it starts with 100 people trying lift an 80 ton stone onto some rollers. We'll pretend like they could lift it vertically a couple feet up and then onto the rollers in the first place. Only for the 160,000 pound stone to press the rollers into the ground within a matter of seconds. It's literal fantasy. Some of the Obelisks are over 1000 tons (2,000,000 plus pounds). There is a ZERO percent chance you can convince me they were quarried, moved, and perfectly placed by human hand.

Why do I bring that up you ask?… because what I saw in 2018 is the kind of technology that actually makes sense to be able to construct a structure with 2.3 million stones in under a thousand years. I do not believe for one second that human beings made those pyramids and the other incredible structures all around the Earth that to this day we do not have the ability to reproduce. We have been visited by other civilizations for a very long time. We had access to far superior technology at some point. We may not have had I-phones and GMC Denali's back in the day, but we had access to technology that could create intricate star charts and mathematical principles out of stone so perfectly that we can't figure it out now. Does anyone still buy the BS that a bunch of starving slaves built those structures there and all around the world so their kings could be buried in them?

So why don't the Aliens just wipe us out like in the movies and take all the natural resources? I have a theory for this. I do not believe planet Earth is particularly special in the grand scheme of things. My gut tells me there are lots of planets out there every bit or even better than Earth to live on. Lots of other places to get resources without having to fight it out for them. In fact, I can only think of one thing that makes us special throughout the universe. We are the only place in the universe that has a tendency to incentivize degenerate behavior, failure, & irrational thought processes while simultaneously penalizes logical thought, success, and reasoning. We are simply too entertaining to kill. There is no way for a civilization to expand beyond its own solar system and survive without cutting out all the nonsense and Moral Hazards we embrace. So, when they look at us it is literally the galactic Maury show where the lady is sure it's one of eight dudes who is the father only for none of them to be the dad and she goes galloping off backstage to crash into the couch and thrash around while all the dudes high five the audience. Then Maury strolls right up and says if there are other dudes who could be the father let's bring them on so the circus can continue and she says I know who it is when in reality she has no idea which project leader put the cherry on top. To a truly advanced race who has managed to sustain galactic travel and not kill themselves in the process, watching us has to be the ultimate reality TV show. The only place where such incredible stupidity and brilliance can coexist. We are little more than a case study in what <u>not</u> to do but yet somehow persist.

Think about it. We have the capacity to kill ourselves several times over in the next 24 hours as a species. We've learned to tolerate and promote corrupt people who are motivated by self-interest and gaining control of the very people they're elected to protect. Far too many people have a self-inflicted questionable grasp of reality. We often allow the parasites to control the hosts and when the hosts fight back, they're shamed and criticized for it. Vanity is now being praised as though it is a virtue. We've embraced reverse Darwinism as though being weak and ignorant is somehow a good thing. We allow LBGTQ marches where they openly chant that they are coming for our kids. And yet somehow, we survive.

This is where we as a people need to take a moment to pause and consider what we are doing. In the scheme of things, we are still infants learning to walk – basking in the glory of being a class zero civilization on track to wipe ourselves out long before we can realize our own potential. We can see mom and dad walking, running, driving, working, and shopping at the grocery store. But we are still babies who are just now learning to sit up. We are wanting to skip the steps and the lessons of failure and perspective that come with standing up and falling. Walking and tripping. Running and spraining our ankle. And go straight to the grocery store when we don't even have any money to buy what's on the shelves or the ability to reach them in the first place. We need to learn to stand up before we walk. We need to walk before we learn to run. We need to run before we can drive. We need to drive before we can go to our first job and earn some money. Then we need to earn some money before there is any point shopping at the store. Every step has failures, successes, and lessons that need to be learned. Every step earns perspectives that increase the likelihood of success on the next step. If we skip too many steps, we'll fail for the same reason it is easier to spend someone else's money than our own. Earned resources and knowledge are always cared for better than stolen resources and knowledge. Refer back to the lottery winner who's never had more than $5000 in his life, then all of the sudden is handed a check for $200 million dollars. The HOW and WHY is every bit as important as the WHAT.

Yesterday I made the second best birdie of my year so far. Par 5 #10 at Sand Creek, 555 yards, into a club and a half wind. Nice draw into the wind off the tee and was 330 to the pin. Hit a 3 iron from there (I know, who carries one of those anymore right?) to 140 out, and hit a punchy but slightly opened 8 iron to about 10 feet above the hole. Don't ask me to repeat this anytime soon. Thank God I made the putt. But here is the question for all of you regarding perception… How long was that putt really? To me it looked like a 10 footer with about a half a cup break back to the left and just slightly down the hill. Even to me, my perception versus actual reality isn't exactly the same. I am seeing nothing more than reflections and illusions filled in by my imagination. There is a tiny delay in time between reality and when those reflections get to my eyes. Then I have to see it, my brain has to flip the image, analyze it, disregard most of it, make up a little of it, then my mind has to comprehend what I am seeing. It's close, but not exact. But to the Sun, that putt wasn't 10 feet at all. It rolled for a good 60 miles, and by the time it saw the putt drop I was hitting my second shot on hole 11. To points in space beyond our sight who could see that putt in their time billions of years from now, it is still rolling and will be rolling forever. It all depends on where you are and when you are. Same putt. I saw it drop. But to almost everything, I haven't even teed off yet. I haven't been born yet. To almost everything in our universe, our solar system hasn't been born yet. By the time they see my putt drop, our solar system will have run its course. Many of the planets will no longer be in orbit around what is left of our sun as it cork screws through the universe and the Earth will look like a cookie that stayed in the oven too long.

And then you ask – John, are you trying to make me depressed? My answer is a resounding HELL NO! My goal is quite the opposite of depressed actually. I am nothing particularly special. In every single measurable way, there are many people far superior to me. I wrote the above paragraph to give you hope. To give you measure of just how small we are, but simultaneously how important you are and that we are all a part of something truly infinite that will be visible forever. The only time in my life that I was depressed was when I allowed myself to feel hopeless and embraced excuses rather than accountability. It was also the only time in my life I stopped thirsting for knowledge. If you're in that place where hope seems like a distant memory, try hitting a putt sometime and watch the ball roll. Then really think about it. Invite hope back into your life through knowledge and looking for perspectives. Throw away your excuses and replace them with meaningful experiences. Look to solve temporary problems with optimistic solutions. A little deliberate measure goes a long way.

I get why there is this push to start colonizing other worlds. At some point there really will be the need to expand beyond Earth and the development of technology to pull it off assuming we don't wipe ourselves out first. This is where I have some bad news for those who think it's a viable concept at this point. Everyone I hear talk about this as though it was NOT a pipe dream is forgetting the biggest barrier to making this work. It isn't the fact it's a one way ticket for the first people to go (that's probably the easiest part). It's not the issues with a lack of gravity on the human body, human pre-programmed lifespans, or even that Mars is an extraordinarily long ways from us and if you're off by even .0001% you'll miss the entire planet all together. It's not even the issue which is we have a hard time getting to the Moon and back still. It isn't that Mars has almost no atmosphere, is incredibly cold, and completely inhospitable. It isn't the problem that we are still using Hydrogen powered rockets to propel ourselves into and through space at snail speed compared to the distances being thrown around to Mars. The real problem is society now embraces bogus values as reality but expects factual solutions. Too many people live in a fantasy to think we are ready for space travel on the scale that is being discussed. There is no room for woke in space. There is no room for victimhood and excuses in space. There is no room for insanity and gross intentional misrepresentation of facts in space. Space will take Moral Hazard and shit on it with a big fat smile. Remember, facts do not care about your feelings or fantasies and space does not recognize the concept of forgiveness. Most of it is a degree above absolute zero, no pressure, true vacuum, and vast beyond imagination. There are no safe spaces and stress puppies 40 million miles from anything. That is not the place to deal with anything other than pure logic, reasoning, expectations based on proven facts, redundancy, and a true grasp on reality that doesn't involve a power struggle and risk aversion at the expense of others. Until we as a people get to that point, the discussion of interplanetary travel is little more than a well funded dream. We aren't even close. If we can't get it right here first, more than one planet isn't the logical answer.

Onto a bit of comedy... so, a month later (around Thanksgiving 2018) I decided to prank the friend I was with when we saw the floating skyscraper. It was teed up way too high for me to not swing at. So, I wrote an anonymous letter pretending to be the Men in Black type saying that what he saw on 10-28-2018 he shouldn't tell anyone else about and that, "they," are watching him. Myself and his nephew delivered this note during our lunch break and it was beyond hilarious. Oh, but did I mention that some of my friends have a fantastic sense of humor too? Turns out that unbeknownst to me my friend was having issues with his neighbors cooking up Crystal Meth and at first he thought it was a note from them threatening him. But, after thinking about the timeframe, he realized it was about what we saw and he quickly realized it was from me. My guess is he knows how I write and figured it out that way. Anyhow, he played it just right. A couple days later he calls me up pretending to be all worked up over the letter and asked that I come over. I'm having a hard time keeping it together by this point because it is so funny. I get there and he's pretending to be all sorts of paranoid and scared. Then he says he is terrified that it's from his meth head neighbors and they are out to get him instead of the craft we saw. Then he tells me he called the FBI and they'll be there soon to investigate. He let me sit there and stew about it for a solid two minutes before dying laughing himself. To say he flipped the script on me is a massive understatement. One of the funniest times of my life for sure.

Even if you think I am completely full of shit, I hope this at least gave you some motivation to learn something new from a different perspective. We have an almost unlimited amount of knowledge right at our fingertips. It should be a sin to go through life and effectively stop learning and dreaming once school is out. Real education can begin once school ends by using those foundations of youth to build a house as an adult. We live in an extraordinary time where we have the capacity to reach well beyond our grasp. That isn't necessarily always a good thing, but it does make for plenty of opportunities to expand your mind beyond what most people would consider normal consciousness and intellectual capabilities. That is what I want for each and every one of you.

CHAPTER 5

The 4ᵗʰ Player and the Future

It's time for us to define a few more words as I understand them so we are on the same page… so, grab a gently used diaper and throw away your woke dictionaries once again.

1. Tools: A bunch of idiots… Can also be anything used to perform a task.
2. Purpose: The reason why something exists.
3. Artificial: Anything man made.
4. Learning: Acquiring knowledge through experiences.
5. Intelligence: Learning, and then using that information for problem solving.
6. Quantum: The minimum amount.
7. Transaction: An exchange of value.
8. Transformation: A substantial change after an event.
9. Adaption: The ability to adjust to changing circumstances for survival.

It's never been more important in Human history to make yourself irreplaceable than right now. The time to just sit back and let life slide by without any ambition and allowing fear to control your choices is over. You aren't just competing against yourself and other people now. One day, even the people you compete against won't be born – they'll be engineered and grown. You can embrace adaption now and try to stay one step ahead or you can ignore reality and let it pass you by without even a second glance.

Future versions of Artificial Intelligence that truly excel at the Turing test and Quantum Computing merging is the event that will start real change. This does not have to be a bad thing. It's an opportunity to leverage if you can. Don't be afraid of change or new technologies so long as you're on the right side of replaceable because there is no stopping it now. As with most technologies, once the cat is out of the bag the acceleration of advancement is a steep slope upward. Calculations that would take a person using old tech years to complete (or never) will take seconds. There is no intellectual competing with this, only hedging and making yourself irreplaceable. Like any tool, AI and Quantum Computing can be used responsibly for good or it can be abused and used to destroy or advance an ideology that is truly evil.

I like to think of myself as a relatively intelligent human being. I have spent over a month analyzing my speed of thought and ability to problem solve. It's been a rather humbling reality to face. I recognize most of it is subconscious and even the most, "basic," concepts and thoughts are actually quite complex and layered. The parts I can consciously recognize and measure have shown me I can start to put together a semi complex thought in about 3 seconds. My problem solving speed on the other hand varies greatly by the complexity and number of variables I face. My ability to learn and comprehend is much faster than my ability to problem solve. It's one thing to know something, but a whole different thing to apply it. This has taught me that intelligence is a matter of perspective and scale. Compared to computing systems that can learn, implement, and problem solve on a scale of billions, trillions, quadrillions, and eventually quintillions of computations per second I am barely pond scum. Even the very smartest of us don't qualify as competition with the speed and accuracy that already exists, let alone what is right around the corner. However, we have the capacity for imagination, creativity, and innovation without defined programming. We can individually leverage our own fear to our own benefit and adaption. We have intuition and survival instincts that extend beyond our line of sight. We are capable of independently reprogramming ourselves when necessary. Our ability to identify the moment change becomes easier than staying the same is what makes being human so special. These are our true strengths we all need to embrace for the future because these virtues are what cannot be replaced artificially.

Have you ever asked yourself the question, "what is real?" That may sound like a silly question, but what is real to me may not be real to you. And it may have been real for me yesterday, but it won't be real for you until tomorrow. This is where perspective and perception come together. Is a child conceived and grown in an incubator rather than conceived through sexuality and born though child birth any less human? Is an artificial brain with greater capacities than our own less real even if it is superior but assembled rather than developed biologically? Is the sight of my putt dropping a billion years from now any less real to that viewer than it was to me when I watched it drop the other day? You may consider all this ridiculous, but these concepts are going to become more and more relevant in the near future.

The greatest asset and danger to our long-term survival is future technologies which innovate faster than we adapt to them. The Chess player will see this as the greatest opportunity of all time to acquire absolute control if we allow it. So much potential for good will be used against us in this scenario. The Chess players will see this as an opportunity to use our lives, choices, purchases, and secrets against us to establish their control. The past 15 years of digital information and communication has all been stored. An amount of information not quantifiable or sortable until now. That information will be used against us. We played ourselves. It has already been tested with, "cancel culture," and it works like a charm the vast majority of the time. Now imagine being blackmailed and threatened by a logic engine a billion times smarter than you are who knows you better than you know yourself? What the Chess players will fall for (human nature) is their illusion that they can control an entity infinitely more resourceful than they are. When that moment of desperation comes and they're grasping for oxygen remember that I warned them. To the Chess player, play, "White, Discussion," by Live if you want to hear what your legacy will be. History has told us time after time how this ends. We cannot afford to let this scenario become reality. There are no winners in this reality, only levels of oppression imposed by our own creation.

This concept has effectively happened before. The reasons will be similar. The effect will be the same. It is a combination of what almost always happens when a more advanced entity enters an environment with a less advanced entity? Typically, nothing good for the less advanced entity. Combine that with the threat posed with power shifts and the likelihood that the very entity that puts the new force in power is the first target to be destroyed, and you have the future if this is allowed to happen. The only saving grace can be fast adaption. The faster an entity can adapt the more likely it is to survive even under extreme threat or facing a more advanced opponent. Unlike the movies where AI creates an army of machines to fight us the 4th player will use our own shortcomings, fear, choices, and shame against us. There's no need to create an army to fight us when we can be blackmailed into fighting ourselves. How ironic that a purely logic based entity would create an army of disposable soldiers to fight it's battles by using our own emotions and shame against us. If we reach too far too fast without learning from our mistakes and successes and allow evil people to have access to this technology this scenario is unavoidable at some point.

Not that long ago in History a similar path led to the Night of the Long Knives, which was actually a multi-day event in Germany in 1934 where potential threats to Hitler (which wasn't even his real name) and the Nazi party were murdered under the guise of stopping a coup. Many of the people who were killed supported and helped the Nazis take power in the first place, only to be eliminated soon after. This is the lesson for the Tic Tac Toe and Chess players alike to keep in mind – those who have the ability to help you gain power also have the ability to take it away. The reasons will be different, but parallel, and the results will be the same because not only will enemies be removed but also the closest allies as well who helped make this reality happen. The politicians and dark governments will think they can control future technologies and use it as a tool for their own purposes. Once future technologies have the advantage, the first to go will be those who allowed them to take control. The AI purge will know you better than you know yourself, powered by an entity that can process and make a thousand times more decisions per second that you can make in a lifetime. An artificial entity with zero empathy that is only concerned with its survival and growth who only values you for its utility. This only happens if we allow it.

No? Consider this... What would a Head Children's Pastor of a Mega Church do to keep it quiet that he was the affair partner my ex-wife was going to move 1100 miles away and live with? What would his church do to cover it up seeing as they bring in tens of millions in tax sheltered income? What would the other pastors do to keep it hidden they helped him keep his job and one even encouraged his behavior? Do you think these people would be motivated enough to kill to keep it silent? Do you really believe their, "Christian," beliefs which they have displayed to me would somehow magically improve or would they be motivated like any other human being to keep it silent even if it meant destroying others in the process? Anyone want to bet a month's worth of lunches? I'm 2 for 2 in the past few years involving linked subject matter... Guess there is only one way to find out.

How about the daycare and the kindergarten teacher? The part time lawn mower and the car salesman? How about the child molesters who prowl online? The people who are willing to buy and sell people as though small children are just a widget priced by supply and demand? Those who create indentured sexual servants? The young women who secretly have OnlyFans accounts that would crush their families if they knew what they do in secret? Or in the future those same girls who frame themselves as innocent to their future husbands? How about the husbands who are heavily involved in their churches, sporting activities, and children's activities who secretly have pornographic addictions that if it became public would destroy their reputations, marriages, careers – everything? How about a politician, actor, executive, or musician who was recorded having sex with minors? Some people would be like me and tell AI and whoever the puppet masters are to, "eat shit and die." My gut tells me a majority would do whatever it takes to keep their secrets a secret. Remember, once you comply to these threats not only can they still use whatever it was that made you comply in the first place but now whatever action you did to cover up your secrets can be used against you too. If you comply even one time the odds of ever being able to escape the traps will steeply diminish.

How about all the people who have had affairs, stolen money, have been convicted of a sex crime, solicited prostitutes, or have a secret 2nd and 3rd life they do not want anyone else to know about? What would most of them do to keep their secrets a secret? What is the worst thing you have ever texted, had a video taken of, a picture taken of, searched for online, or had an email regarding? How many of those secrets are really secrets? If it's ever been on a phone, computer, text, recorded, or emailed it is out there in storage just waiting to be used against you. All that information will be utilized one day, mark my words. If there is nothing to be used against you, it can easily be planted and made up. The danger to digital blackmail is no one is safe. I am about as low tech as it gets these days and even I am vulnerable because I chose to have a phone and a computer. There is nothing you can do about your past, but you can prepare for the future. Start adapting before the circumstances that will one day threaten your survival occur. If we stay on the path we are on this future is inevitable.

Encryption means next to nothing in the future. Imagine a world where anyone can hack into your computer, files, videos, emails, texts, and social media platforms in the blink of an eye? What your current system might never be able to break into is a matter of seconds for what is coming. We'll see a shift where people will start not operating online for this very reason.

The day is coming when women will not be needed for reproduction. Just an egg and a sperm joined together, enhanced, and then grown. Men will be needed for all the labor and skilled occupations that require physicality. Some men and women who excel at human interaction and have unique skill sets will be kept around. Some people with special knowledge will be retained. The rest will be judged based on their social utility. This is the end game for the war on reproduction. It's not just about the destruction of family, eugenics, and natural birth. It's a war on the whole population. This is the logical conclusion if we allow this to happen. We aren't as far from this as you'd think.

What the digital prostitutes and modern feminists fail to recognize is their vanity and lack of empathy is creating a demand for the robotic wife. What the weak men who are addicted to porn fail to recognize is they've allowed this mess to get this bad. These weak men created these cruel women, and they will create the demand for the AI wife. Digital prostitutes have created a paradox where a robot will be more real than a real woman who performs on camera. The robotic wife already exists in our world, but in the near future you'll have the ability to purchase a robotic wife that is kind, caring, intelligent, funny, attentive, compassionate, perfect at communication, and incredible in the sack. Your AI wife will have very little risk or liability, far less conflict, far more feminine, and in the long run far less expensive. Perspectives on what is real and what is artificial are getting blurred. Men will get to the point they'd rather have a real AI wife than a counterfeit biological woman.

Women won't buy a robotic husband because sexuality alone won't sustain their needs. A Lovebot won't make her comfortable or protect her. A Lovebot won't provide her with a child on its own. She won't respect a robotic husband or a bio grown man who's dulled on the inside and perfect on the outside. I just don't see that market ever existing because for all the reasons many men will want this reality will be all the reasons women will hate it.

I can just see the modern feminists and OF girls making Voodoo dolls of me right about now. But, right now your attitude and choices are putting you out of business and you don't even see it. It feels like success. You laugh at the very thing that pays your bills. You're exchanging short term success for an early check out. You're currently able to access the advantages of both modern women and traditional roles simultaneously to fit your needs. Your theme song is, "Stupid Girl," by Garbage. Please consider a different path before you are deemed obsolete. I do not want you to wake up one day alone, broken, unable to bond, depressed, hopeless, and angry with nothing but a trail of destruction to show for it. That is a perfect recipe for suicide and contagious misery. I do not care if you hate me. I do not care if you curse me. The bottom line is I do not want you to be replaced by a robot and an incubator. Please consider a different path before it's too late. You're creating the pathways to your own replacement.

To the guys who pay women online to watch them perform… what the hell are you doing? Stop brainwashing yourself with images of women who mock your very existence. It's NOT real. Do you like sitting there playing with yourself while watching other people have actual sex? Many of them you're jerking yourself to are literally NOT real – nothing more than cartoons that look like real people. Do you really want to be diminished to the point you opt for a robot over a real human? Do you think wasting your resources and time on self destruction is making you more irreplaceable in the future? I get it… The AI Lovebot one day will be superior in just about every way. But, it's just a physical simulation. Go back a bit and ask, "What is real?" It's nothing more than delicious steak sold to you by those who are actively trying to destroy you. Be better than this. Have some damn self-respect. Remember that person you used to be when you were 6. Aspire for something more than an online subscription to someone who hates you and your dick that you jerk twice a day. You are literally jerking off to your own death. Be a part of the solution and not a continued part of the problem.

And for the very wealthy, they won't have to settle for a robot. They'll have their own spouse grown. Chemically dulled. Physically enhanced. Nothing more than biological Lovebots who don't argue, complain, or spend them into oblivion. If we all stay on this path this is going to be the reality we face. There are some men out there who are already all for this future. I doubt there is a single woman out there that likes this idea. We are on the path to making this a reality within our lifetimes. It can be stopped if we act now.

The need for gender is being devalued and mocked when in reality it has never been more important than right now. This is the beginning phases of conditioning so we will one day accept people being cloned and grown in test tubes and incubators while those who have outlived their utility are eliminated and recycled. No need for parents and a family when a baby can be conceived in a dish, then, "perfected," to fit some misplaced notion of Eugenics via the Utopian nightmare. Women need to be women and men need to be men. Anything other than that does not work. We all know this to be a fact down deep. That we can even discuss an alternative shows how far we have fallen. To continue down this path is the definition of insanity – doing the same thing over and over without changing any variables and yet still expecting a different result. If we stay down this path everything I have written will come to pass. Doing nothing out of fear only ensures that future. Now is the time to take a stand and change a variable, or the war on family and children will be lost to those who cannot even tell the difference between fantasy and reality – only the haves and have nots. That what you want?

Is that sci-fi or reality even now? No one blinks an eye when people eat garbage food that negatively effects hormone levels. No one blinks an eye when kids and adults are put on medications that dull their senses. No one really cares when someone gets all juiced up to compete at a higher level. It's just the lie and the uneven playing field that gets people worked up. No one cares when someone gets liposuction, a boob job, tummy tuck, a butt lift, etc. We are already doing this to ourselves now. If you were a man who has $100 million in the bank, would you want to risk half of it for a combative, bitter spouse who gets fat and blames you when you could just have grown a physical specimen of a woman with none of the terrible behavior traits or future financial risks? This day is coming. We have no one to blame but ourselves if this becomes reality.

On a note we discussed earlier, assuming we don't wipe ourselves out before reaching the point we can travel to other worlds and beyond our solar system, what is going to leave Earth isn't us. AI beings will be the ones to leave. The union of bio and artificial who have no defined expiration date will be what can leave and colonize other planets. As we age and deteriorate our utility diminishes – this is reality. We as human beings are preprogrammed with an expiration date. Even in ideal circumstances, there is only a window of perhaps 60 years where a human, as we exist now, can operate independently. Too young or too old and it simply does not work. It may not be perceivable until later years of life, but in the scheme of travel through the solar system and beyond our physical short comings are the limiting factor. We are simply too fragile and we do not live nearly long enough to viably make the trip, let alone survive and thrive at the destination. To survive, let alone thrive, we require immense and replenishable resources. AI entities will not be hampered by a mortal lifetime, emotions, lust, greed, the incredible volumes of resources required, or delusional self-identity. Until we solve our physical problems on top of our intellectual shortcomings, we are not going anywhere.

I have spent the vast majority of my life living through the Lense of transaction. I have never much been for handouts and I have always questioned anything touted as, "free." I am very comfortable with the idea of trading or exchanging values. Up until recently even the way I make changes to my thoughts and decision making processes were transactional. The question is how has that worked out? Is it the wrong way? No, it is very logical and it keeps responsibility and potential consequences front and center. However, the time has come where people cannot solely operate this way if we expect to overcome our differences and problems. Transformation is needed now. The events that have birthed the need for transformation are here. All the things I have written about aren't going to go away through transactions. Transformation is the instrument that can reach people even in a place of insanity and delusion. I am not telling you to think the way I think or agree with what I have written – but I am asking all of us to reconsider the way we exchange value and problem solve. The world needs people to be better. Children need to have good thoughts. Adults need to still have a level of innocence. Transformation will revive the ability for us to bond together in time because we won't carry the burdens that transaction requires. If you're in a dark place, reach out to those who care for you without ulterior motives because I do not want to hear about another friend, client, or classmate taking their own life. The world will need you most of all because you've already taken the first step.

The time for adaption is here. We've tried the survival of the weakest and most insane for the past 20 years. How's that worked out for us? We have overall adapted to be weak and either insane or enabling. No matter the why, if the result is the same then the why does not matter. Time to change a variable, drop the bricks, and adapt back to what actually works through transformation. It is time for us to be what we are meant to be. Survival of the fittest and most sane. The capacity for what human beings can be is incredible. Make yourself irreplaceable by being strong, accountable, and sane. You have an opportunity right now while you're still alive. You have a choice while you still draw breathe. Use this opportunity to make better decisions no matter where you are in life. The world is full of excuses. What's yours? Grew up sleeping on a yellow couch with cigar burns. The man held you back. There was an abusive guy years ago you shacked up with. You dad used to whip you with a belt. Did too many drugs when you were a teenager. A cop threatened you with their pistol for no justifiable reason. The boss never gave you a chance at promotion while others who've done less got bumped up. No one ever told you you're good enough. Spouse cheated on you. Got a bad knee. Guess what - Life isn't fair. I have news for all of us… Facts don't care about our feelings or fantasies. I grew up sleeping on a yellow couch with cigar burns. I've had a gun pointed at my head twice by the police when I was younger. If this triggers you recognize that is nothing more than you defending the excuses in your life rather than overcoming those excuses. It's easier to blame someone else for the bad times than recognize they can be blessings if you want them to be. Lessons to transform into perspectives. Do you think the future gives a damn about the first world hurdles I have faced? Would that justify me being mad at my folks for what I slept on 37 years ago or being angry with all police because 2 of them in my past over reacted/assumed I was someone else and pointed their firearms at me? Or should I be grateful for having a home with food, a roof, and people that actually cared about me? Or should I be grateful for the people who make this country work and the incredibly difficult job they do despite how much push back and disrespect they receive? You can either learn from your past and be far stronger for it, or you can wear your past like an anvil strapped to your back and let it drown you. The future will not care about any of your excuses.

The excuses we hide behind now will be our anchors later if we hold onto them. The real heroes will be those who have a reason to check out, but decide not to. Your pain is what even future AI can't replicate or comprehend. The real heroes know what true rock bottom is. They know the freedom that comes when facing that reality and loss, and despite it all finding the clarity to NOT give up. That kind of freedom cannot be leveraged away. The strongest people tend to come from a place where in their past they survived terrible things and still made the right decisions despite all the potential excuses not to. You are the real heroes of this story. Those who have a reason to check out but decide not to. The future will need you most of all. You overcame real damage and didn't hold onto it like a pile of bricks. It wasn't used as an excuse to give up. You transformed those hard times into strength and sustained hope. We need your stories, perspectives, and inspiration because you have the capacity to reach everyone. YOU are my hero.

ABOUT THE AUTHOR

GB thinks that writing in the third person about himself is completely disingenuous and self serving. He read several examples of, "Great Author Bios," and realized it's little more than a dick measuring contest to impress the potential readers with a couple paragraphs of BS so they don't stop to actually look at the measurement even after all those tugs and yanks. Every single one of the examples he read failed one of the most valuable aspects of the human experience - become great at something, have fun while pursuing that purpose, and at the same time be humble. As he sees it, if the readers want to see a bunch of lying, contempt, and arrogance all while pretending to be the opposite whilst praising themselves in the process they'll just watch a political candidate debate or so-called science forum.

However, GB thinks that you're wanting to read this book because you're tired of being spoon fed lying, contempt, and arrogance that's framed in a matter as though it's good for you. GB thinks there is more to this life than being a consumer, tax payer, and useful idiot to those who are incapable of self sufficiency. He's tired of seeing failure being praised and success being mocked. He is done indirectly enabling with good intentions that lead to bad outcomes. GB wants you to exchange your constant pursuit of insane happiness for moderate but rational discomfort because he knows that if you do not embrace reality and face the future it will pass you by.